Stories to Teach Islamic Manners to Kids

Allah's Guidance for Good Manners

Aasma S.

My First Picture Book Inc.

Copyright © 2024 by My First Picture Book Inc.

All rights reserved.

No portion of this book may be reproduced in any form without written permission from the publisher or author, except as permitted by U.S. copyright law.

Contents

Introduction	1
1. The Magic Words: Saying Bismillah	4
2. Thank You, Allah: The Power of Gratitude - Alhamdulillah	8
3. Please and Thank You: The Best Words - Adab	12
4. Sharing is Caring: The Gift of Generosity - Sadaqah	16
5. Kindness Counts: Helping Others in Need - Ihsan	20
6. Forgiving Heart: The Story of Forgiveness - Afw	24
7. Respect Your Parents: Love and Obedience - Birr al-Walidayn	28
8. Greeting with a Smile: The Sunnah of Salam - Assalamu Alaikum	32
9. Speak Gently: The Power of Words - Lisan Tayyib	36

10.	Clean Little Muslim: Importance of Cleanliness - Taharah	40
11.	The Honest Trader: A Tale of Truthfulness - Sidq	44
12.	Patience is Beautiful: The Story of Waiting - Sabr	48
13.	Fairness First: Treating Everyone Equally - Adl	52
14.	Lend a Helping Hand: Being There for Others - Khidmah	56
15.	Keeping Promises: The Value of Trust - Amaanah	60
16.	Generous Hearts: Giving to Charity - Zakat	64
17.	Humility in Every Step: A Lesson in Modesty - Tawadu	68
18.	Being On Time: Respecting Appointments - Waqt	72
19.	Respecting the Elders: A Story of Courtesy - Ihtiram	76
20.	No Bullying Allowed: The Story of Empathy - Rahmah	80
21.	Caring for the Earth: Protecting Allah's Creation - Khilafah	84
22.	A Friend in Need: The Importance of Friendship - Ukhuwwah	88
23.	Respecting Personal Space: A Story of Boundaries - Hudud	92

24.	Thank You for Your Hard Work: Appreciating Others - Shukr	96
25.	The Truth Always Wins: Speaking the Truth - Haqq	100
26.	Helping Hands at Home: A Story of Responsibility - Masooliyyah	104
27.	Modesty in Dress: A Lesson in Islamic Attire - Haya	108
28.	Listening with Care: The Value of Attention - Insat	112
29.	Kind Words to Animals: A Lesson in Mercy - Rifq	116
30.	The Power of Dua: Always Asking Allah - Dua	120
31.	Standing Up for Justice: A Brave Little Girl - Qist	124
32.	Using Time Wisely: The Story of Productivity - Barakah	128
33.	Respecting Others' Beliefs: A Story of Tolerance - Tasamuh	132
34.	The Golden Rule: Treating Others as You Want to Be Treated - Ma'ruf	136
35.	Control Your Anger: The Power of Calm - Hilm	140
36.	Use Your Ears First: The Lesson of Listening - Sama'	144

37.	Guard Your Tongue: Think Before You Speak - Hifz al-Lisan	148
38.	The Blessing of Water: Not Wasting It - Ni'mah	152
39.	Visiting the Sick: A Sunnah of Compassion - Iyadah	156
40.	Quiet in the Mosque: Respecting Allah's House - Adab al-Masjid	160
41.	Learning with Love: The Importance of Knowledge - Ilm	164
42.	A Clean Heart: Avoiding Jealousy and Hatred - Niyah	168
43.	Gentle with the Young: The Sunnah of Caring - Rifq al-Sighar	172
44.	Respecting Property: A Lesson in Integrity - Amanah	176
45.	Fulfilling Promises: A Trustworthy Muslim - Wafa'	180
46.	Gratitude in Hard Times: A Story of Faith - Shukr al-Haal	184
47.	Don't Waste Food: The Story of Blessings - Ni'mat al-Ta'am	188
48.	Helping Your Siblings: The Bond of Brotherhood - Ukhuwwah	192

49. Don't Be Greedy: Sharing What You Love - Ithar   196

50. The Art of Apology: Saying Sorry When Wrong - Tawbah   200

Introduction

Welcome to **"Stories to Teach Islamic Manners to Kids - Allah's Guidance for Good Manners!"** In this special book, you will explore wonderful stories that show how Allah's teachings can guide us to live a good, kind, and respectful life. Just as a light shines in the dark, Allah's guidance helps us see the right path and make good choices every day.

The Quran, our holy book, is filled with wisdom and lessons that teach us how to be the best we can be—by showing kindness, speaking truthfully, helping others, and treating everyone with respect. These stories bring to life the values that Allah loves and encourages in all of us. They remind us that good manners are more than just polite words; they are a way to show love and gratitude to Allah and make the world a more beautiful place.

Through these stories, you will learn how to act with compassion, be honest in your actions, and show respect to everyone around you.

Each story is like a small treasure from the Quran, guiding us to live in harmony with others and be the best version of ourselves, just as Allah wishes for us.

As you read, think about how you can practice these manners every day, whether at home, at school, or with friends. Remember, every small act of kindness and respect brings us closer to Allah and fills our hearts with His love.

We hope these stories inspire you to follow Allah's guidance and make a positive difference in the world around you. Happy reading, and may Allah bless you with goodness always!

Happy reading and learning!

Chapter 1

The Magic Words: Saying Bismillah

Ibrahim woke up early one sunny morning, eager to start his day. He hurried to the kitchen, where his mother, Amira, was preparing breakfast. Without thinking, Ibrahim grabbed his spoon and began to eat his cereal. The spoon slipped from his hand, and milk splashed onto the table. The cereal bowl tipped over, spilling the contents across the table.

Amira gently reminded him, "Saying '**Bismillah**' before starting to eat helps us remember Allah and brings blessings."

Ibrahim listened carefully, nodding his head. His mother explained, "Bismillah means 'In the Name of Allah.' We say it to ask for Allah's help and blessings before doing anything, like eating, drinking, or even playing."

Later that day, Ibrahim went outside to play with his favorite red ball. He kicked the ball high into the air, but instead of landing back near him, it bounced over the fence and rolled into a bush. The ball got stuck among the branches, and Ibrahim struggled to pull it out. He pulled and tugged, but the ball didn't move.

At that moment, his sister Layla walked by. She saw Ibrahim struggling and asked him, "Did you say 'Bismillah' before you started playing?"

Ibrahim shook his head. Layla smiled and suggested, "Try saying 'Bismillah' now, and then pull the ball."

Ibrahim said, "Bismillah," softly and then tugged on the ball again. This time, the ball came out easily. Surprised and happy, Ibrahim looked at his sister, who nodded with a smile.

The next morning, when Ibrahim sat down for breakfast, he remembered his mother's words. Before picking up his spoon, he said, "Bismillah." This time, nothing spilled, and Ibrahim enjoyed his breakfast peacefully.

At school, Ibrahim shared his lunch with his friends. Before taking a bite, he said, "Bismillah," just as he had learned. His friend Ali, curious, asked, "Why do you say that before eating?"

Ibrahim replied, "It means 'In the Name of Allah.' It helps us remember Allah and brings blessings."

Ali decided to join him, and together they said, "Bismillah," before eating their sandwiches. The food tasted even better, and they both felt happy.

Later that afternoon, Ibrahim went to the park with his father. There was a tall slide that looked exciting but also a little scary. Standing at the top, Ibrahim felt a bit nervous. He remembered Layla's advice and whispered, "Bismillah," before sliding down. The slide was thrilling, and Ibrahim's fear disappeared. He enjoyed the ride so much that he went up and slid down many more times.

As the days passed, Ibrahim continued to say "Bismillah" before doing anything important. Whether it was eating, playing, or trying something new, he felt more confident and at peace. His parents noticed how Ibrahim was growing, not just in his actions but also in his heart, as he remembered Allah in everything he did.

Saying "Bismillah" had become a part of Ibrahim's daily life, making each moment more special and blessed.

Moral of the Story: Always say "Bismillah" before starting anything to ask for Allah's blessings and help.

Chapter 2

Thank You, Allah: The Power of Gratitude – Alhamdulillah

Amina loved her bicycle. One sunny afternoon, she decided to ride around her neighborhood. She pedaled fast, feeling the breeze on her face. As she turned the corner, her bike wobbled, and suddenly, the chain came off. Amina tried to fix it, but her hands were too small to put the chain back on. She felt upset and sat down on the curb, not knowing what to do.

Her father noticed her sitting sadly and came over. He asked, "What happened, Amina?"

"My bike's chain came off, and I can't fix it," Amina replied.

Her father gently smiled and said, "When something goes wrong, remember to say '**Alhamdulillah**.' It means 'All Praise is due to Allah,' and it helps us remember to be thankful, even when things don't go our way."

Amina listened carefully and decided to try. She softly whispered, "Alhamdulillah," and took a deep breath. Her father showed her how to fix the chain. With a little help, Amina's bike was ready to go again. She felt happier and decided to continue her ride.

Amina rode to the park, where her friends were playing soccer. She joined the game and kicked the ball hard, but it went the wrong way and missed the goal. Her friends groaned, and Amina felt embarrassed. She stood still for a moment, feeling bad.

Then, she remembered her father's words. She closed her eyes and said, "Alhamdulillah," even though she missed the goal. She decided to keep trying and play her best. The next time she got the ball, she aimed carefully and kicked it again. This time, the ball flew straight into the goal! Her friends cheered, and Amina felt proud and happy.

Later, Amina saw an ice cream truck parked by the playground. She ran over with her friends, excited to get her favorite chocolate ice cream. But when she reached into her pocket, she realized she didn't have any money. Amina felt disappointed. Her friends bought their ice creams, and she stood there, feeling left out.

Just then, she remembered to say "Alhamdulillah." Even without the ice cream, she was thankful for being with her friends and enjoying the day. As she said the words, her friend Yasmin came over and handed her a small cone of chocolate ice cream.

"You can have mine, Amina!" Yasmin smiled.

Amina's face lit up with joy. "Thank you, Yasmin!" she exclaimed, and took a small bite. "Alhamdulillah," she whispered, feeling grateful for her friend's kindness.

On the way back home, dark clouds started to gather in the sky, and it began to rain. Amina didn't have an umbrella and started to feel worried. She remembered her mother's words about being thankful. She whispered, "Alhamdulillah," for the rain because she knew it was a blessing from Allah. Soon, her father arrived with a big umbrella to take her home.

At dinner that night, Amina sat with her family. Her mother asked, "How was your day, Amina?" Amina smiled and said, "It was good! I learned to say 'Alhamdulillah' even when things didn't go right. It made me feel better, and everything turned out fine."

Her parents smiled proudly. Amina felt happy in her heart, knowing that saying "Alhamdulillah" helped her feel thankful and see the good in every situation.

Moral of the Story: Always say "Alhamdulillah" to show gratitude to Allah, even when things don't go as planned, and trust that everything will work out for the best.

Chapter 3

Please and Thank You: The Best Words – Adab

Yusuf was excited to build a tall tower with his new set of colorful blocks. His sister, Sara, was sitting nearby, reading a book. Yusuf needed some help to find the red blocks, which were his favorite. Without thinking, he shouted, "Sara, give me the red blocks!"

Sara looked up, surprised. She didn't like the way Yusuf had asked, so she shook her head and went back to her book. Yusuf felt upset and grumbled.

Yusuf's mother noticed his frustration and asked, "Yusuf, did you say 'Please' when you asked Sara for help?"

Yusuf looked puzzled and replied, "No, I just told her to give me the blocks."

His mother smiled gently and explained, "In Islam, we show '**Adab**' by using kind words like 'Please' and 'Thank You.' It makes others feel respected and happy to help. You should try asking again, but this time, say 'Please.'"

Yusuf thought for a moment and decided to give it a try. He turned to Sara and asked nicely, "Sara, could you please give me the red blocks?" Sara smiled back and handed him the blocks right away.

Yusuf felt happy. He added the red blocks to his tower, and this time, it stood tall and strong. He clapped his hands with joy and said, "Thank you, Sara!"

Sara replied, "You're welcome, Yusuf!" and went back to her book with a big smile on her face.

Later, Yusuf went to the kitchen to grab a snack. He saw a plate of cookies on the counter. He reached out to take one, but his mother stopped him. "Yusuf, remember to ask first," she reminded him.

Yusuf thought again about what his mother had said earlier about adab. He asked, "Mom, could I please have a cookie?" His mother smiled and gave him a cookie. Yusuf took a bite and felt the sweet chocolate melt in his mouth. "Thank you, Mom!" he said happily.

When it was time to go outside, Yusuf wanted to play with his friend Ali's new soccer ball. He ran over to Ali and said, "Give me the ball!" Ali frowned and held the ball closer to himself. He didn't like how Yusuf had asked.

Yusuf remembered his mother's advice about showing adab. He took a deep breath and tried again, saying, "Ali, may I please play with your ball?"

Ali's frown turned into a smile. "Sure, Yusuf! You can play with it," Ali replied, passing the ball to Yusuf. They both played and had a great time kicking the ball back and forth.

Before going home, Yusuf handed the ball back to Ali and said, "Thank you for letting me play with your ball." Ali grinned and said, "You're welcome, Yusuf! Let's play again tomorrow."

That night, Yusuf sat with his family for dinner. He was happy about his day. He had learned how saying "Please" and "Thank You" and practicing adab made everyone around him feel good. His mother smiled and patted his back, saying, "You see, Yusuf? Kind words and showing adab are like magic; they make everything better."

Yusuf nodded. He felt proud and knew he would always use these polite words from now on.

Moral of the Story: Using polite words like "Please" and "Thank You" is part of showing adab, which reflects respect and kindness to others and makes everyone happy to help.

Chapter 4

Sharing is Caring: The Gift of Generosity - Sadaqah

Fatima had a beautiful doll with a blue dress and shiny black shoes. It was her favorite toy, and she played with it every day. One afternoon, her friend Aisha came over to play. Aisha saw the doll and asked, "Can I play with your doll, too?"

Fatima hesitated. She loved her doll and didn't want anyone else to touch it. She shook her head and said, "No, it's mine." Aisha looked disappointed, but she didn't say anything. They played with other toys, but Aisha didn't seem as happy. Fatima noticed but didn't understand why.

The next day at school, it was time for recess. Fatima brought some tasty cookies her mother had baked. They were chocolate chip, her favorite! She started eating them, and Aisha came over and asked, "Can I have one of your cookies, please?"

Fatima quickly hid the bag and said, "No, I don't want to share." Aisha looked sad and walked away to play with other friends. Fatima felt a little bad but continued eating her cookies alone.

As the days passed, Fatima noticed Aisha started playing with other children. When they sat together, Aisha was quieter and didn't seem as excited as before. Fatima began to feel lonely and wondered what was wrong.

One day, Fatima's teacher, Mrs. Rahma, told the class a story about **'Sadaqah'**, which means giving and sharing with others. She explained that sharing with friends is a kind act that makes everyone happy. Fatima listened carefully and thought about what the teacher said. She realized that maybe she hadn't been very kind to Aisha.

After school, Fatima decided to try something new. She took her favorite doll with her and went to Aisha. "Would you like to play with my doll today?" Fatima asked with a smile.

Aisha looked surprised but very happy. "Really? You're going to share your doll with me?" she asked.

Fatima nodded. "Yes, I want to share it with you," she replied. They both played with the doll, taking turns and laughing together. Fatima felt a warm feeling in her heart. It felt good to see Aisha so happy.

The next day, Fatima brought her cookies to school again. This time, she went straight to Aisha and said, "Would you like to share my cookies with me?"

Aisha's face lit up with a big smile. "Yes, thank you, Fatima!" she exclaimed. They sat together, enjoying the cookies, and talking about their favorite games. Fatima realized how much more fun it was to share her treats and toys.

From that day on, Fatima made sure to share her toys and snacks with her friends. She noticed that when she shared, her friends were happier, and they all had more fun together. Whenever she shared, her heart felt light and joyful.

One day, her teacher noticed Fatima's new behavior and said, "I see you are learning to share, Fatima. Sharing is a beautiful way to practice Sadaqah, and it brings happiness to everyone."

Fatima felt proud. She realized that sharing wasn't just about giving away things but about making others feel good and creating more joy around her.

She understood that a little generosity could make a big difference, and she felt thankful for learning the true meaning of Sadaqah.

Moral of the Story: Sharing with others makes everyone happy and shows kindness and generosity.

Chapter 5

Kindness Counts: Helping Others in Need - Ihsan

One Saturday, Khalid was playing soccer in his backyard. He kicked the ball hard, and it flew over the fence into his neighbor Mr. Ahmed's garden. Khalid knew that Mr. Ahmed was an older man who had trouble bending down. Khalid climbed over the fence to get his ball. He saw Mr. Ahmed trying to pick up some leaves but struggling to do so.

Khalid thought, "I should help him," but then he hesitated. He wanted to keep playing soccer with his friends and felt shy about offering help. He quickly grabbed his ball and ran back without saying anything.

The next day, Khalid went outside to ride his bike. As he passed by his friend Samir's house, he saw Samir trying to fix the chain on his bike. Samir looked frustrated. Khalid thought about stopping to help but decided to keep riding. He told himself, "I want to enjoy my ride now. Maybe I'll help him later."

That afternoon, Khalid's mother asked him to help her carry groceries from the car. Khalid complained, "But I'm busy playing!" His mother sighed and said, "Khalid, helping others is a way to show kindness. It is called '**Ihsan**' in Islam. It means doing good for others, even when you don't feel like it."

Khalid thought about his mother's words. He remembered Mr. Ahmed struggling with the leaves and Samir trying to fix his bike. He felt bad for not helping when he had the chance. Khalid decided he would try to do better next time.

The following day, Khalid saw Mr. Ahmed outside again. This time, Mr. Ahmed was trying to water his plants, but the watering can was too heavy for him. Khalid quickly ran over and said, "Mr. Ahmed, can I help you with that?"

Mr. Ahmed smiled warmly and handed the watering can to Khalid. "Thank you, Khalid," he said. "That is very kind of you." Khalid felt happy as he watered the plants, and he realized that helping others made him feel good inside.

Later, while riding his bike again, Khalid saw Samir still struggling with his bike chain. Khalid stopped and asked, "Do you need some help, Samir?" Samir nodded eagerly. Khalid got off his bike and helped him fix the chain. It was a bit tricky, but they managed to do it together.

"Thanks, Khalid!" Samir said with a big grin. "Now I can ride my bike again!" Khalid felt a warm glow in his heart. He was glad he stopped to help his friend.

The next morning, Khalid woke up early and decided to help his mother without being asked. He helped carry the groceries, set the table for breakfast, and even watered the plants in the garden. His mother smiled and said, "I see you are learning the true meaning of Ihsan, Khalid. Helping others brings peace and happiness, both to them and to you."

Khalid realized that by helping others, he felt much happier, and everything around him seemed better. He learned that a small act of kindness could make a big difference in someone's day. He decided he would always look for ways to help, knowing that his kindness would bring joy to everyone around him.

Moral of the Story: Being kind and helping others, even in small ways, makes everyone happy and brings peace and joy to our hearts.

Chapter 6

Forgiving Heart: The Story of Forgiveness - Afw

Maryam loved to draw. She had a special sketchbook where she kept all her favorite drawings. One day, during art class, she brought her sketchbook to school to show her friends. Her friend, Zayn, asked if he could look at it. Maryam agreed and handed it over carefully.

Zayn flipped through the pages, admiring the pictures. But then, by accident, his hand slipped, and a page tore. Maryam's favorite drawing of a beautiful butterfly was ruined. She felt a surge of anger and quickly snatched the book back. "Why did you do that?" she shouted, feeling upset.

Zayn's face turned red. "I'm so sorry, Maryam. I didn't mean to," he said softly. But Maryam was too upset to listen. She put her sketchbook away and didn't speak to Zayn for the rest of the day.

The next day, Maryam continued to feel upset. She didn't sit with Zayn at lunch, and she ignored him during recess. Zayn looked sad and tried to apologize again, but Maryam turned away.

Later, during a game of catch, Maryam saw Zayn playing alone. She remembered how much fun they used to have playing together. She missed laughing and sharing stories with him. But she still felt hurt about her drawing.

That afternoon, their teacher, Mrs. Noor, read a story about forgiveness. She explained that in Islam, forgiveness is called **'Afw'**. It means letting go of anger and showing kindness, even when someone makes a mistake. Maryam listened closely. Mrs. Noor added, "When we forgive others, it makes our hearts light and brings peace to everyone."

Maryam thought about what her teacher said. She realized that her heart felt heavy because she was holding onto her anger. She missed Zayn's friendship and wondered if forgiving him would make her feel better.

After school, Maryam walked over to Zayn, who was sitting alone on a bench. She took a deep breath and said, "I'm still upset about my drawing, but I forgive you, Zayn. I know you didn't mean to tear the page."

Zayn's face brightened. "Thank you, Maryam! I'm really sorry. I was going to draw a new butterfly for you," he said, pulling out a piece of paper with a colorful butterfly he had drawn.

Maryam smiled. "It's beautiful!" she said, feeling her heart lighten. They both laughed and promised to play together again.

The next day, during art class, Maryam felt happier. She noticed how much fun it was to have Zayn as a friend again. She also realized that forgiving him had made her feel better.

A few days later, Maryam was playing in the playground when she accidentally bumped into Aisha, spilling Aisha's juice all over her new dress. Aisha looked upset, but Maryam quickly said, "I'm so sorry, Aisha! I didn't mean to."

Aisha looked at Maryam, then smiled. "It's okay, Maryam. I forgive you." Maryam felt grateful and happy.

Maryam realized how important it was to forgive others, just like Aisha had forgiven her. She felt proud to have learned the power of a forgiving heart, or Afw. She decided she would always try to forgive, knowing it would bring peace and happiness to everyone.

Moral of the Story: Forgiving others when they make mistakes helps us feel happier and keeps our hearts light and full of peace.

Chapter 7

Respect Your Parents: Love and Obedience – Birr al-Walidayn

Omar was very excited about his new toy car. It was shiny, fast, and had flashing lights. One day, he came home from school, eager to play with his car. His mother was in the kitchen, trying to prepare dinner. She saw Omar rushing past and called out, "Omar, can you please help me set the table?"

Omar stopped and frowned. "But I want to play with my new car," he said. He ignored his mother's request and ran to his room.

As he played with his toy car, he heard a loud crash from the kitchen. He ran back and saw that a bowl had fallen off the counter, and his mother looked tired from cleaning up the mess. Omar felt a little guilty, but he still wanted to play with his car. He went back to his room, thinking, "I just want to have fun."

Later that evening, his father came home. He asked Omar, "Did you help your mother today?" Omar shook his head and said, "I was too busy playing." His father looked serious and said, "Omar, helping your parents is important. In Islam, it's called **'Birr al-Walidayn'**. It means respecting and obeying your parents."

Omar listened but still didn't feel like he had done anything wrong. He just wanted to play. The next day, Omar's toy car stopped working. No matter how much he pushed, it wouldn't move. He tried to fix it but couldn't. He felt sad and frustrated. His mother noticed and came over.

"Omar, if you had helped me yesterday, I might have had time to help you fix your toy," she said gently.

Omar realized his mistake. He thought about his father's words and felt bad for not helping his mother. He decided to make things right.

The next morning, Omar saw his mother carrying a heavy laundry basket. He quickly ran over and said, "Mom, let me help you with that." His mother smiled, surprised but happy. Together, they folded the clothes and put them away.

Later, his father asked him to help water the plants in the garden. Omar remembered what his father had said about Birr al-Walidayn. He nodded and replied, "Yes, I will help you, Dad." They worked together, watering the plants and pulling out weeds. His father smiled and said, "Good job, Omar. You're learning to be a good son."

That evening, as they sat down for dinner, Omar's father handed him a small wrench. "Let's fix your toy car together," he said. Omar's face lit up with joy. He watched closely as his father showed him how to tighten the screws and check the wheels. Soon, the car was zooming across the floor again, lights flashing brightly.

Omar felt happy and proud. He realized that helping his parents made everyone feel better, including himself. He understood that respecting his parents wasn't just about listening to them but also about showing love and care.

From that day on, Omar made sure to help his parents whenever he could. He cleaned up his room, helped his mother with cooking, and listened carefully to his father's advice. He felt happier and noticed that his parents seemed happier, too.

Omar learned that Birr al-Walidayn, respecting and helping his parents, brought peace and love into their home. He decided he would always try to be a good son, knowing that it was the right thing to do.

Moral of the Story: Always respect and help your parents, as it brings love and happiness to the whole family.

Chapter 8

Greeting with a Smile: The Sunnah of Salam - Assalamu Alaikum

Zain loved going to school, but sometimes, he felt a little shy around his classmates. One morning, Zain walked into his classroom quietly and went straight to his seat. He didn't greet anyone, and his face looked serious. His friends, Aisha and Omar, were playing a game, but they didn't notice Zain.

When the teacher, Mrs. Fatima, asked a question, Zain raised his hand to answer. But before he could speak, another student, Ali, was called on instead. Zain felt a little upset. "Why didn't anyone notice me?" he wondered.

At lunchtime, Zain sat by himself, feeling lonely. He watched the other kids laughing and talking. He wished he could join in, but he didn't know how. He kept thinking, "Why doesn't anyone want to play with me?"

Later that day, Zain saw the janitor, Mr. Ahmed, cleaning the hallway. Zain noticed that Mr. Ahmed looked tired. Zain remembered that his parents always greeted people with a smile and said, "**Assalamu Alaikum**," which means "Peace be upon you."

He decided to try it. Zain walked up to Mr. Ahmed, smiled, and said, "Assalamu Alaikum, Mr. Ahmed!" Mr. Ahmed looked up, surprised, and smiled back. "Wa Alaikum Assalam, Zain," he replied with a cheerful voice. "Thank you for greeting me! You just made my day brighter."

Zain felt a warm feeling inside. He realized that just a small greeting made Mr. Ahmed happy. He decided to try it again.

The next morning, Zain walked into the classroom with a big smile. He said, "Assalamu Alaikum" to his friends Aisha and Omar. They looked up and smiled back. "Wa Alaikum Assalam, Zain!" they replied. Aisha invited him to play their game. Zain felt happy and joined in, laughing and playing with them.

During recess, Zain noticed a new student sitting alone. The boy looked a little scared and didn't know anyone. Zain walked over with a big smile and said, "Assalamu Alaikum! My name is Zain. Would you like to play with us?"

The new student's face brightened. "Wa Alaikum Assalam! I'm Sami," he replied, feeling welcomed. Zain introduced Sami to his friends, and soon, they were all playing and laughing together. Zain realized how a simple "Assalamu Alaikum" made someone feel included and happy.

As the days went by, Zain greeted everyone he met with "Assalamu Alaikum" and a big smile. He noticed that more people greeted him back and that his friends wanted to play with him more. Even his teacher, Mrs. Fatima, smiled and said, "Zain, I see you are greeting everyone with a smile and Salam. This is a beautiful Sunnah, a practice of the Prophet Muhammad (peace be upon him). It spreads peace and happiness."

Zain felt proud. He understood that greeting others with "Assalamu Alaikum" was not just about saying words. It was about spreading peace, love, and happiness to everyone around him.

From that day on, Zain made it a habit to greet everyone he met with "Assalamu Alaikum" and a bright smile. He learned that a small greeting could make a big difference in someone's day and bring people closer together.

Moral of the Story: Greeting others with "Assalamu Alaikum" and a smile spreads peace and happiness to everyone around you.

Chapter 9

Speak Gently: The Power of Words - Lisan Tayyib

Aisha was playing in the schoolyard with her friends during recess. She was building a sandcastle when her friend, Sara, accidentally bumped into her and knocked it over. Aisha felt a surge of anger and yelled, "Why did you do that? You're so clumsy!" Sara looked hurt and quickly walked away, her eyes filling with tears.

Aisha felt annoyed and went back to building her sandcastle, but now she felt lonely. The other children saw how Aisha had shouted at Sara, and they chose to play somewhere else. Aisha was left by herself, feeling upset. "Why is everyone avoiding me?" she wondered.

When she returned to class, Aisha noticed that no one wanted to sit near her. She felt sad and confused. During lunchtime, she tried to join another group of friends, but they seemed distant and didn't talk much to her. Aisha felt hurt and didn't understand why everyone was acting this way.

After school, Aisha's teacher, Miss Layla, noticed Aisha sitting alone. Miss Layla talked to Aisha and explained, "Aisha, in Islam, it is important to use kind words, or '**Lisan Tayyib**'. It means speaking gently and avoiding hurtful language. Words can hurt others' feelings, just like they have hurt Sara today."

Aisha remembered how she had shouted at Sara and felt bad. She realized her words were not gentle or kind. She wanted to make things right. The next day, Aisha saw Sara sitting alone in the playground. She felt nervous but decided to go over and apologize.

"Sara," Aisha said softly, "I'm sorry for yelling at you yesterday. I didn't mean to hurt your feelings."

Sara looked at Aisha and smiled. "Thank you, Aisha. I forgive you," she replied. Aisha felt relief and happiness. She realized that using kind words helped make things better.

Later, during art class, Aisha was working on a painting. Her friend, Yusuf, asked if he could borrow her blue paint. Aisha remembered Miss Layla's words about Lisan Tayyib. She smiled and said, "Sure, Yusuf, here you go!" Yusuf grinned back and said, "Thanks, Aisha! You're always so nice."

Aisha felt proud. She realized how much nicer it felt to use kind words. During the rest of the day, Aisha continued to speak gently to everyone. She complimented her classmate's drawing, thanked her teacher, and said "Please" and "Thank you" whenever she asked for something.

By the end of the day, Aisha noticed that her friends were happier around her. They invited her to play and talk, and she felt more included. She saw how her gentle words made a big difference.

That afternoon, when she got home, Aisha helped her little brother with his homework. He struggled with his math, and instead of getting frustrated, Aisha said, "You're doing great! Let's try this together." Her brother smiled, feeling more confident.

Aisha felt proud of herself for using gentle and kind words. She learned that speaking kindly, or Lisan Tayyib, brought peace and happiness to everyone around her, including herself.

From that day on, Aisha decided to always speak gently and use kind words, knowing they had the power to make people feel loved and appreciated.

Moral of the Story: Using gentle and kind words makes everyone feel happy and loved, and it brings peace to our hearts and those around us.

Chapter 10

Clean Little Muslim: Importance of Cleanliness - Taharah

Bilal loved to play outside. One day, he was having fun in the park with his friends. They played tag, ran around, and climbed trees. After playing, Bilal's clothes were dirty, and his hands were covered in mud. He felt tired and hungry, so he decided to go home for lunch.

When Bilal reached home, his mother was setting the table for lunch. He rushed to the table and tried to grab some bread with his muddy hands. His mother stopped him and said, "Bilal, your hands are dirty. You should wash them before eating."

Bilal frowned. He was too hungry and didn't feel like washing his hands. "I just want to eat now," he complained.

His mother shook her head and said, "In Islam, being clean is very important. It's called '**Taharah**'. It means keeping ourselves and everything around us clean. Cleanliness is a big part of our faith."

Bilal sighed but didn't listen. He started eating without washing his hands. Soon, his stomach began to feel uncomfortable, and he didn't feel so good. He realized that the dirt on his hands had mixed with his food. He felt bad and decided to go to his room.

Later that day, Bilal wanted to pray. He went to his prayer mat, but his clothes were still dirty from playing in the park. His sister, Amina, saw him and said, "Bilal, your clothes are dirty. You need to be clean to pray properly."

Bilal felt a bit embarrassed. He remembered his mother's words about Taharah. He went to his mother and said, "Mom, I want to pray, but my clothes are dirty. What should I do?"

His mother smiled and replied, "First, wash your hands and face properly. Then, change into clean clothes. Being clean is important when we pray because it shows respect to Allah."

Bilal nodded and went to the bathroom. He washed his hands, face, and feet carefully, making sure there was no dirt left. He changed into fresh clothes and felt much better. He prayed with a clear heart and a clean body.

The next day, Bilal went to school. He noticed that his desk was messy with papers and pencil shavings. His teacher, Miss Nadia, walked by and said, "Bilal, keeping your desk clean helps you find things easily and shows respect for the classroom."

Bilal remembered what he had learned about cleanliness. He decided to tidy up his desk. He threw away the scraps, organized his books, and wiped his desk with a clean cloth. His classmates noticed and started cleaning their desks too.

By the end of the day, the whole classroom looked neat and tidy. Miss Nadia smiled and said, "Thank you, Bilal, for helping everyone keep the classroom clean."

Bilal felt proud. He realized how important Taharah, or cleanliness, was not just at home but everywhere. He noticed that being clean made him feel happier, healthier, and more comfortable.

From that day on, Bilal always made sure to wash his hands before eating, wear clean clothes, and keep his surroundings tidy. He learned that Taharah was not only important in Islam but also made everyday life better for everyone.

Moral of the Story: Keeping ourselves and our surroundings clean brings happiness, health, and respect to everyone.

Chapter 11

The Honest Trader: A Tale of Truthfulness - Sidq

Amir loved playing with his friends at the park every weekend. One Saturday, his friends decided to set up a lemonade stand to raise money for new soccer balls. Amir was excited to join them and help. They squeezed fresh lemons, added sugar, and poured the lemonade into big cups. It was a hot day, and they were sure many people would want a cool drink.

The stand became busy quickly. People were lining up, and Amir was in charge of pouring the lemonade into cups. While serving, he accidentally knocked over the lemonade pitcher, spilling some on the table. Only a little lemonade was left. Amir realized they might not have enough for all the customers.

A woman came up and asked for two cups of lemonade. Amir felt worried because he knew there wasn't much left, and some of it might be too watery after the spill. He decided not to say anything and poured two cups, trying to hide the fact that they were half-filled and watery. The woman paid and took the cups, but Amir felt uneasy.

Next, a man came up and asked for a cup. Amir poured the last of the lemonade, knowing it was mostly just water by now. The man took a sip and frowned. "This lemonade tastes very watery," he said.

Amir felt his face turn red. "Oh, I'm sorry," he stuttered, but the man didn't look happy and walked away.

Feeling guilty, Amir knew he had made a mistake by not being honest about the lemonade. He remembered what his father had taught him about '**Sidq**' in Islam, which means truthfulness. Amir decided he needed to make things right.

He called over his friends and explained what had happened. "I think we should be honest with our customers," he said. "We should tell them that the lemonade is running low and might be watery."

His friends agreed, and they decided to refill the pitcher with fresh lemons and sugar. When they were ready, a woman came by and asked, "Is your lemonade still good?"

Amir replied, "We had some trouble earlier, but now it's fresh again. Would you like to try it?"

The woman smiled and said, "Thank you for being honest. I'll take a cup." She tasted it and nodded, "This is delicious!" She bought two more cups for her children.

More people came to the stand. Amir and his friends made sure to be truthful about the lemonade. They told everyone that they had just made a fresh batch and that it tasted much better now. The customers appreciated their honesty, and soon the stand was busy again.

Later, the man who had been unhappy returned. He said, "I heard you made a fresh batch of lemonade. Can I try it again?" Amir nodded, poured a cup, and offered it with a smile. The man took a sip and smiled back. "This is much better! Thank you for being honest this time," he said.

Amir felt a wave of relief and happiness. By the end of the day, they sold all their lemonade and raised enough money for the soccer balls. Amir realized that being truthful made everyone happier and made their lemonade stand a success.

Moral of the Story: Always be honest, even when you make a mistake, because truthfulness brings trust and makes things better for everyone.

Chapter 12

Patience is Beautiful: The Story of Waiting - Sabr

Layla loved to bake cookies with her grandmother. One day, her grandmother planned to bake a special batch of chocolate chip cookies for Layla to take to school and share with her friends. Layla was excited and couldn't wait to start.

As they mixed the dough, Layla wanted to taste it immediately. "Can I have a little now?" she asked, but her grandmother shook her head. "Not yet, Layla. We need to wait until the dough is ready," she replied. Layla frowned but decided to wait, even though it was hard.

They finished mixing, and it was time to put the cookies in the oven. Layla kept peeking inside, eager to eat them. After just a few minutes, she asked, "Are they done yet?" Her grandmother smiled and said, "No, Layla, you need to wait a little longer. Good things take time."

Layla felt impatient, but she tried to wait. She looked at the clock, watching the seconds tick by. She wanted the cookies right now. She paced around the kitchen, feeling frustrated. "Why is it taking so long?" she thought.

Finally, she could not wait anymore. Layla opened the oven door too early, and some of the cookies slid off the tray, landing on the oven door. "Oh no!" Layla cried. She felt upset, realizing her mistake. Her grandmother gently closed the oven and said, "Layla, we must practice **'Sabr'**, which means patience. Let's clean up and try again."

Layla felt bad, but she listened. They carefully put the cookies back on the tray and placed them in the oven again. Her grandmother said, "Let's find something fun to do while we wait." They decided to play a game and told each other stories. Layla found herself laughing and enjoying the time with her grandmother. She wasn't thinking about the cookies anymore.

After a while, the timer finally went off. Her grandmother took out the cookies, and they smelled delicious. Layla felt proud that she had waited patiently this time. She realized that it wasn't so bad to wait after all.

The next day, Layla brought the cookies to school. Her friends were excited to try them. But just as they were about to eat, Layla's teacher announced, "We have to wait for a few minutes; it's time for a school assembly."

Layla saw her friends looking disappointed. Some of them sighed and groaned. Layla remembered what she had learned about Sabr, or patience, and decided to help. She said, "Let's play a guessing game while we wait! It will make the time go faster."

Her friends agreed, and soon they were all laughing and guessing. Before they knew it, the assembly was over, and they could finally eat the cookies. Everyone loved them and thanked Layla. She felt happy and realized that being patient made everything better.

That evening, Layla told her grandmother about her day. Her grandmother hugged her and said, "See, Layla? Patience is beautiful, and it always brings something good in the end."

Layla nodded, understanding the lesson about Sabr. She knew now that waiting calmly and staying positive, even when things didn't go her way, made her feel better and brought joy to everyone around her.

Moral of the Story: Practicing patience, or Sabr, helps us stay calm and happy, even when things take time or don't go as planned.

Chapter 13

Fairness First: Treating Everyone Equally - Adl

Amina loved to play games with her friends at school. One day, during recess, she decided to organize a game of tag. A group of kids quickly gathered around her, excited to join in. Amina noticed that her friend Zayd, who was a fast runner, wanted to play, but so did Noor, who was slower because of her short legs.

Amina wanted her team to win, so she chose Zayd first. Then she picked her other friends who were also fast runners. Noor looked hopeful, but Amina hesitated and picked someone else instead. Noor's smile faded, and she ended up on the last team, feeling a little sad. Amina didn't notice and started the game with her fast team.

The game began, and Amina's team quickly took the lead. They were winning, and Amina felt happy. But she noticed that Noor was having trouble keeping up, and her team was losing. Noor tried her best, but she couldn't run as fast as the others. Some kids started to giggle, and Noor's face turned red. She seemed upset, and Amina realized she had made her friend feel bad.

After the game, Amina saw Noor sitting by herself. She remembered what her parents had taught her about '**Adl**', which means fairness in Islam. Amina thought about how she hadn't been fair by only picking the fastest runners for her team.

The next day, Amina decided to do things differently. She wanted everyone to have fun, so she suggested a different game: a relay race where everyone had to take turns. This way, it didn't matter who was the fastest because everyone had a chance to participate.

As they divided into teams, Amina made sure to mix the fast runners with the slower ones. She picked Noor first this time and encouraged everyone to do their best, no matter how fast or slow they were.

The race began, and the playground filled with laughter. Noor's turn came, and she ran as fast as she could. Her teammates cheered for her, and Amina shouted, "Go, Noor, go!" Noor smiled brightly and did her best. When the race ended, it didn't matter who won; everyone was clapping and cheering for each other.

Later, during snack time, Noor came up to Amina and said, "Thank you for being fair today, Amina. I had so much fun!" Amina felt a warm feeling in her heart and realized how much better it felt to treat everyone equally.

That afternoon, Amina saw a group of kids playing hopscotch. She noticed that one of her friends, Fatima, was shy and standing on the side. Amina invited her to join the game and made sure everyone took turns, no matter how good they were at hopping. Everyone smiled and played together, enjoying the game.

Amina learned that being fair, or practicing Adl, made all her friends feel happy and included. From that day on, she made sure to treat everyone equally, whether they were fast runners or slow, confident or shy.

By the end of the week, Amina noticed that everyone seemed to be having more fun at recess. She felt proud and knew she had done the right thing by treating all her friends fairly, just as she had learned from the teachings of Adl.

Moral of the Story: Being fair and treating everyone equally makes everyone feel happy and included, no matter their abilities or backgrounds.

Chapter 14

Lend a Helping Hand: Being There for Others - Khidmah

Ismail enjoyed riding his bike around his neighborhood every day. One day, he noticed his elderly neighbors, Mr. and Mrs. Ali, standing outside their home looking worried. A large tree branch had fallen in their driveway after a storm the previous night, blocking their car. Mr. Ali tried to move it, but it was too heavy for him.

Ismail saw them from across the street. He thought about helping but remembered he had planned to go to his friend's house to play with his new action figures. He hesitated and decided to ride away, thinking, "Maybe someone else will help them."

Later that week, Ismail rode by again and saw Mrs. Ali struggling to carry a big box from her porch. Ismail knew he could help, but he was eager to get home to watch his favorite cartoon. He felt a bit guilty as he rode past, but he told himself he would help next time.

That evening, Ismail's mother asked him, "Ismail, did you see Mr. and Mrs. Ali today? They seem to have a lot to do lately."

Ismail nodded and replied, "Yes, but I was busy. I'll help them next time." His mother smiled gently and said, "You know, Ismail, in Islam, helping others is called '**Khidmah**'. It means showing kindness through our actions. It's important to help others, especially our neighbors."

Ismail felt a bit embarrassed. He knew his mother was right. He decided that next time, he would try to be more helpful.

The very next day, Ismail saw Mr. Ali trying to put up a ladder to clean the gutters on his house. The ladder was tall and wobbly, and Mr. Ali looked like he was struggling to balance it. This time, Ismail didn't hesitate. He put down his bike and ran over to help.

"Can I hold the ladder for you, Mr. Ali?" Ismail asked. Mr. Ali smiled in relief. "Thank you, Ismail! That would be very helpful," he replied. Ismail held the ladder steady while Mr. Ali climbed up and cleaned the gutters safely.

When they were done, Mr. Ali said, "I don't know what I would have done without your help today, Ismail. Thank you!" Ismail felt a sense of pride and happiness inside.

The following morning, Ismail saw Mrs. Ali in her garden with her hands full of flowers, trying to find a place to plant them. She looked confused and tired. This time, Ismail ran over and said, "Mrs. Ali, do you need any help planting those flowers?"

Mrs. Ali smiled warmly and replied, "Yes, Ismail! I was trying to decide where to plant them. Could you help me dig some holes over there?"

Ismail nodded and quickly got to work, digging holes and helping Mrs. Ali plant the flowers. She thanked him with a big smile.

That afternoon, Mr. Ali brought over a plate of homemade cookies for Ismail and his family. "This is for you, Ismail, to thank you for all your help," he said. Ismail felt proud and realized that lending a helping hand, or practicing Khidmah, was not only important but also made him feel good inside.

From then on, Ismail made it a habit to check on Mr. and Mrs. Ali regularly, offering to help whenever he could. He understood that Khidmah meant being kind and helpful, even when it wasn't always convenient.

Moral of the Story: Helping others, especially those who need it, is a kind and important action that brings joy to everyone.

Chapter 15

Keeping Promises: The Value of Trust - Amaanah

Noor loved spending time with her friends at the playground after school. One day, she promised her friend Aisha that she would bring her favorite board game, "The Animal Safari," to school the next day so they could play together during recess. Aisha was excited and said, "I can't wait! Thank you, Noor!"

The next morning, Noor was in a hurry. She quickly packed her school bag and rushed out the door. As she walked to school, she suddenly remembered, "Oh no! I forgot to bring the board game!" She thought about going back to get it, but she didn't want to be late for school, so she decided to leave it.

At recess, Aisha ran up to Noor with a big smile. "Did you bring the game?" she asked eagerly. Noor looked down and said, "I'm sorry, Aisha. I forgot to bring it."

Aisha's smile disappeared, and she looked disappointed. "But you promised," she whispered. Noor felt bad but didn't know what to say. Aisha walked away sadly, and Noor realized she had let her friend down.

Later that day, Noor asked another friend, Samir, if she could borrow his favorite colored pencils. "Sure," he said. "Just promise to return them tomorrow." Noor promised, "I will!" and took the pencils home.

The next day, Noor brought the pencils back, but when Samir checked them, he noticed that one was missing. "Noor, where is the red pencil?" he asked.

Noor searched her bag but couldn't find it. "I must have lost it," she admitted. Samir looked upset. "But you promised to return all of them," he said. Noor felt embarrassed and realized that she had broken another promise.

That evening, Noor's mother asked her to help clean her room. "I promise I will, after watching my show," Noor replied. But after the show, Noor got busy playing with her toys and forgot all about her promise. When her mother checked later, the room was still messy.

The next day at school, Noor noticed that her friends seemed distant. Aisha didn't ask her to play, and Samir didn't offer to share his pencils. Noor felt sad and lonely. She realized that not keeping her promises had hurt her friends and made them lose trust in her.

Noor decided she needed to make things right. She went home, found the missing red pencil under her bed, and returned it to Samir the next day. "I'm sorry I lost it, but I found it now," she said. Samir smiled and said, "Thank you, Noor. I'm glad you kept your promise."

Then, Noor brought "The Animal Safari" game to school and handed it to Aisha. "I'm sorry I forgot yesterday," Noor said. "Let's play today!" Aisha's face lit up, and she hugged Noor. "I'm so happy you remembered," Aisha said.

That evening, Noor cleaned her room as she had promised her mother. Her mother smiled and said, "Thank you, Noor. I'm proud of you for keeping your promise."

Noor felt happy and realized that keeping promises, or '**Amaanah**', helped her friends and family trust her again. She decided always to keep her promises, knowing it was the right thing to do.

Moral of the Story: Always keep your promises, as it builds trust and strengthens your relationships with friends and family.

Chapter 16

Generous Hearts: Giving to Charity - Zakat

Hamza was excited because it was his birthday, and his grandparents had given him some pocket money as a gift. He had been saving up to buy a remote-controlled car, the one he saw in the toy store window that could flip and spin. He could already imagine himself playing with it.

After school, Hamza went to the toy store to look at the car. It was shiny and bright, and he counted his money to see if he had enough. As he was counting, he noticed a boy about his age standing outside the store, looking at the toys with longing eyes. The boy's clothes were a bit worn, and his shoes had holes in them. Hamza wondered why the boy looked so sad.

The next day, Hamza saw the same boy sitting outside the school gate. He was with his younger sister, and they seemed to be sharing a small piece of bread. Hamza felt a tug in his heart and realized the boy might not have enough to eat or buy toys.

Later that evening, Hamza's father noticed that he looked thoughtful and asked, "What's on your mind, Hamza?" Hamza told him about the boy he saw at the toy store and outside the school. His father smiled kindly and said, "In Islam, we have something called **'Zakat'**, which means giving to those in need. It's a way to share what we have and help others feel happy too."

Hamza listened carefully and thought about his money. He really wanted the toy car, but he also felt sad for the boy. He decided to buy some snacks from the store the next day and give them to the boy and his sister.

The next morning, Hamza saw the boy and his sister again. He walked over and handed them the snacks. "Here, these are for you," he said, smiling. The boy looked surprised but happy. "Thank you!" he replied, and his sister's face brightened with a big smile.

Hamza felt a little better, but he still thought about the toy car. He only had a small amount of money left now. As he walked to the toy store again, he kept thinking about what his father said about Zakat and helping others. He realized that maybe he could do more.

He turned around and went back home. He gathered some of his favorite toys and clothes that were still nice but that he didn't use much anymore. He put them in a bag and asked his father to take him to the local charity center.

At the charity center, Hamza handed the bag to a lady who worked there. She smiled and said, "These will make many children very happy. Thank you for being so kind." Hamza felt a warm glow inside his heart. He hadn't bought the car, but he felt something much better—joy.

A few days later, he saw the same boy and his sister wearing new clothes. The boy waved at him, and Hamza waved back with a big smile. He felt proud of his choice to help others.

Hamza learned that giving to those in need, or practicing Zakat, was much more rewarding than getting something just for himself. He realized that his small act of kindness had made a big difference.

Moral of the Story: Sharing what you have with others in need brings joy and makes the world a happier place for everyone.

Chapter 17

Humility in Every Step: A Lesson in Modesty - Tawadu

Asiya was excited because she had just won first place in the school art contest. Her painting of a bright, colorful garden with butterflies and flowers was now displayed on the wall of the school hallway. Everyone who passed by admired it, and her friends congratulated her all day long.

Asiya felt proud of her achievement. When she got home, she couldn't stop talking about her painting to her parents, her sister, and even her pet cat. "Did you know my painting won first place?" she said to everyone she met.

The next day at school, Asiya saw her friend Leila looking at the painting. "Isn't it great?" Asiya said with a big smile. "I worked really hard on it, and I knew it would win." Leila smiled back but said nothing.

During art class, the teacher announced, "Today, we will be painting landscapes. Let's help each other and learn new techniques." Asiya felt confident. She had already won a prize, so she thought she didn't need any help.

As the class began painting, Leila quietly asked Asiya, "Can you help me mix the colors like you did for your garden painting?"

Asiya shrugged and replied, "It's easy. You should know how to do it by now," and continued with her own work. Leila looked disappointed but didn't say anything.

Later, at recess, Asiya joined her friends on the playground. She couldn't resist talking about her painting again. "My painting is the best, right?" she asked. Some of her friends nodded, but others stayed quiet. Asiya didn't notice their silence and continued to talk about her achievement.

That afternoon, the art teacher showed everyone their new paintings. Asiya looked at hers and felt proud, but when she glanced around, she noticed other children had done beautiful work too. Leila's painting was especially lovely, with soft colors and gentle brush strokes. It was different from Asiya's, but it was just as beautiful in its own way.

The teacher praised Leila's work and said, "This is a great example of using new techniques. Well done, Leila!" Asiya suddenly felt a little embarrassed. She realized that while she had been busy showing off, others had been quietly learning and improving.

Asiya remembered what her parents had taught her about **'Tawadu'**, which means humility in Islam. She realized that being humble meant not showing off, even when you do something well. It meant appreciating others and learning from them too.

The next day, Asiya decided to do things differently. When Leila asked for help again, Asiya smiled and said, "Of course! Let me show you how to mix the colors." They worked together, and Leila's face lit up with happiness. Asiya felt a warm feeling inside. It felt good to help and be kind.

During lunch, instead of talking about her painting, Asiya asked her friends about their own hobbies and what they enjoyed doing. Everyone started sharing their stories, and they all felt closer and happier.

By the end of the day, Asiya learned that being humble, or practicing Tawadu, was more important than always talking about herself. She saw that everyone had their own special talents and that being modest made her feel even better than winning a prize.

Moral of the Story: Be humble and avoid showing off because everyone has something special, and being kind and modest makes everyone feel happy.

Chapter 18

Being On Time: Respecting Appointments - Waqt

Abdullah was excited because his best friend, Hamza, had invited him to play soccer at the park. They planned to meet at 4 o'clock sharp. Abdullah agreed, saying, "I promise to be there on time!" Hamza smiled and said, "Great! Don't be late!"

After school, Abdullah decided to watch his favorite cartoon. He thought, "Just one episode, and then I'll leave." But the show was so fun that he lost track of time. When he finally checked the clock, it was already 4:15!

"Oh no!" Abdullah exclaimed. He quickly put on his shoes and ran out the door. By the time he arrived at the park, it was nearly 4:30. Hamza was sitting on a bench, looking a bit sad.

"You're late, Abdullah," Hamza said quietly. "I was waiting for you."

Abdullah felt bad and said, "I'm sorry, Hamza. I lost track of time."

Hamza sighed and replied, "I understand, but we missed a lot of playtime. Now I have to go home soon." Abdullah felt guilty for breaking his promise. He realized that his lateness had ruined their plan.

The next day, Abdullah promised his teacher that he would help clean the classroom after school. He knew he had to stay and help because he had given his word. But when school ended, Abdullah saw some friends playing a new game outside. He thought, "I'll just play for a few minutes and then help the teacher."

Abdullah joined the game and soon forgot all about his promise. When he finally remembered and went back to the classroom, his teacher was already cleaning up by herself.

"Abdullah, you promised to help," she said gently but firmly. "When you don't keep your word, it causes problems for others."

Abdullah felt ashamed. He realized he had let down his friend and his teacher because he hadn't been on time or kept his promise.

That evening, Abdullah's father noticed he looked upset. "What's wrong, Abdullah?" he asked. Abdullah explained how he had been late to the park and forgotten his promise to his teacher. His father nodded and said, "In Islam, being on time and keeping promises is part of **Waqt'**, respecting time. It's important because it shows others that we care about them and value their time."

Abdullah thought about his father's words. He decided he would do better and respect Waqt by being on time and keeping his word.

The next day, Abdullah set an alarm to remind himself when it was time to meet Hamza. He left early, arriving at the park right at 4 o'clock. Hamza was surprised and happy. "You're on time today!" Hamza said with a big smile. They played soccer and had a great time.

Later, Abdullah stayed after school to help his teacher, arriving on time and ready to clean. His teacher smiled and said, "Thank you, Abdullah. I appreciate you keeping your promise."

Abdullah felt proud and realized that being punctual and keeping his word made everyone happier. From then on, he made sure to always respect time, knowing that Waqt was important.

Moral of the Story: Always be on time and keep your promises, as it shows respect for others and makes everyone feel valued and happy.

Chapter 19

Respecting the Elders: A Story of Courtesy - Ihtiram

Safiya loved playing outside with her friends every afternoon. One day, she was running and laughing when she saw her grandmother, Nani, trying to carry a heavy basket of laundry to the clothesline. Safiya thought, "I want to keep playing," and continued running with her friends, not stopping to help.

A little while later, Safiya saw her neighbor, Mr. Ahmad, who was an elderly man, walking slowly with his cane. He was struggling to pick up the newspaper from his front porch. Safiya was busy chatting with her friends and didn't pay much attention. Mr. Ahmad managed to pick up the newspaper by himself, but he looked tired.

Later that day, Safiya's mother called her inside and said, "Safiya, I noticed that Nani needed help with the laundry today, but you didn't stop to help her. It is important to show '**Ihtiram**', or respect, to our elders by helping them when they need it."

Safiya felt a little embarrassed. She hadn't thought much about it before. Her mother continued, "Respecting elders means more than just saying nice words. It means showing care through our actions."

The next day, Safiya decided to be more mindful. She saw her grandmother in the kitchen, standing on her toes, trying to reach a jar from the top shelf. This time, Safiya quickly ran over and said, "Let me get that for you, Nani!" Her grandmother smiled and thanked her. Safiya felt good for helping.

Later, when she went outside, she saw Mr. Ahmad again. This time, he was carrying a bag of groceries, and it looked heavy. Safiya remembered what her mother had said about Ihtiram. She walked over and asked, "Mr. Ahmad, can I help you carry that bag?"

Mr. Ahmad's face lit up. "Thank you, Safiya, that would be very kind," he replied. Safiya took the bag and carried it to his doorstep. Mr. Ahmad smiled warmly and said, "You are such a helpful young girl. Your kindness means a lot to me."

Feeling happy, Safiya realized that showing respect through small actions could make a big difference. Later, at the community center, she saw another elderly lady, Mrs. Fatima, looking for a seat. The room was full, but Safiya stood up and offered her seat, saying, "You can sit here, Mrs. Fatima."

Mrs. Fatima smiled and said, "Thank you, Safiya. That is very thoughtful of you." Safiya felt a warm feeling in her heart, knowing she had done the right thing.

The next morning, her grandmother shared the story with Safiya's parents about how kind she had been. Her father looked proud and said, "Safiya, you are learning what Ihtiram truly means. Respecting our elders brings peace and happiness to our community."

From that day on, Safiya made sure to always help her elders, whether it was carrying something heavy, offering her seat, or just listening to their stories. She learned that showing respect, or Ihtiram, was not just about being polite but about caring for others in every way possible.

Moral of the Story: Always show respect to elders by helping them and being kind, as it makes them happy and teaches us the importance of courtesy.

Chapter 20

No Bullying Allowed: The Story of Empathy - Rahmah

Musa enjoyed playing on the school playground with his friends every day. One afternoon, he saw a group of kids gathered around, laughing loudly. Curious, Musa walked over and saw that they were making fun of a new boy named Omar, who had just joined their class. Omar was smaller and a little shy, and he looked very upset as the other kids teased him.

Musa watched for a moment, not sure what to do. He wanted to tell them to stop, but he didn't want to get involved and risk being laughed at too. He turned away and decided to play on the swings instead, pretending he didn't see anything.

Later that day, during art class, Omar was sitting alone, looking sad. Musa felt a little bad for not helping him earlier, but he still wasn't sure what to do. He thought, "Maybe it's not my problem." But deep inside, he felt uneasy.

The next day, the same group of kids started teasing Omar again, this time during recess. They took his backpack and tossed it back and forth, while Omar tried to grab it, looking frustrated and close to tears. Musa saw everything, and his heart began to ache. He remembered what his teacher had taught him about '**Rahmah**', which means empathy and compassion in Islam. It meant being kind to others and understanding their feelings.

Musa realized that if he were in Omar's place, he would feel scared and alone. He decided he couldn't just watch anymore. He gathered his courage, walked over, and said loudly, "Hey, stop it! Leave Omar alone!"

The other kids paused and looked at Musa. "Why should we?" one of them asked.

Musa replied, "Because it's not nice to bully others. How would you feel if someone did this to you?" The kids looked at each other and started to feel a bit guilty. Slowly, they stopped teasing Omar and walked away.

Omar looked at Musa with gratitude in his eyes. "Thank you," he whispered. Musa smiled and said, "No one should be treated that way. Let's play together." Omar nodded, and they began to play a game of tag. Musa noticed how happy Omar seemed now that he wasn't being bullied.

Later, during story time, their teacher read a story about kindness and empathy. She explained how important it was to show Rahmah, to put ourselves in someone else's shoes and treat them with kindness. Musa felt proud for standing up for Omar. He realized that Rahmah was not just about feeling sorry for someone but also about taking action to help.

The next day, Musa invited Omar to join his group of friends at lunch. They laughed, shared their snacks, and played games together. The other kids who had teased Omar also began to include him, realizing how much more fun it was to be kind and friendly.

Over time, Omar became more confident and made new friends. Musa learned that standing up against bullying and showing empathy, or Rahmah, made everyone feel happier and safer.

Moral of the Story: Always stand up against bullying and show empathy and kindness to others, making everyone feel safe and included.

Chapter 21

Caring for the Earth: Protecting Allah's Creation - Khilafah

Zaynab loved to play outside in the park near her house. One sunny day, she was playing with her friends by the pond. As they were having fun, Zaynab noticed that the water in the pond looked dirty. There were plastic bottles, wrappers, and bags floating on the surface. She felt sad seeing the fish swimming around the trash.

Zaynab picked up a stick and tried to poke at some of the trash, but her friends said, "Don't worry about it, Zaynab. It's just garbage." She looked at the mess and thought, "Someone else will clean it up," and continued playing.

The next morning, Zaynab woke up and brushed her teeth. As she let the water run, her mother walked by and said, "Zaynab, turn off the tap while brushing your teeth. We shouldn't waste water." Zaynab quickly turned off the tap, but she didn't understand why it was so important.

Later that day, Zaynab went back to the park with her little brother. They saw a group of people planting trees nearby. Zaynab was curious and asked one of the people, "Why are you planting trees?"

The person smiled and said, "We are planting trees to help the environment. Trees give us oxygen, clean the air, and provide homes for birds and animals. It is part of our duty to protect Allah's creation."

Zaynab listened carefully and thought about what the person had said. She realized that everyone has a responsibility to care for the earth. In Islam, this is called **'Khilafah'**, which means being a steward of the earth. She remembered the trash in the pond and felt a bit guilty for not doing anything about it.

The next day, Zaynab decided to make a change. She gathered some friends and said, "Let's help clean the pond. It's our job to take care of our environment." At first, her friends hesitated, but Zaynab explained, "If we don't do it, who will? Allah has trusted us to be the caretakers of His creation."

They all agreed and started picking up the litter around the pond. They found bottles, cans, and plastic bags. It was hard work, but they didn't give up. When they were done, the pond looked much cleaner, and the fish seemed to swim more freely. Zaynab felt proud and happy, knowing they had done something good.

Later, Zaynab remembered what her mother had said about wasting water. She started being more careful, turning off the tap when brushing her teeth and taking shorter showers. She noticed that little actions could make a big difference.

That weekend, Zaynab and her family went to a picnic in the park. She made sure to pick up all the litter after their meal, reminding her brother not to throw trash on the ground. She explained, "We must keep our environment clean. It's our duty as Allah's stewards on earth."

Her family smiled, and her father said, "I'm proud of you, Zaynab. You're learning what it means to be a true Khalifah, a protector of Allah's creation."

From then on, Zaynab made it a habit to take care of the environment. She understood that small actions, like picking up litter and saving water, could help protect the earth for everyone.

Moral of the Story: Take care of the environment by not wasting resources and keeping it clean, as it is our duty to protect Allah's creation.

Chapter 22

A Friend in Need: The Importance of Friendship - Ukhuwwah

Aliyah was excited about the school picnic. Her class was going to the park for a day of fun, games, and a picnic lunch. She packed her favorite sandwich and a big bottle of juice. She couldn't wait to play on the swings and race with her friends.

At the park, Aliyah quickly ran to the swings and started playing with her best friend, Sara. They laughed and took turns pushing each other higher and higher. But soon, Aliyah noticed that her friend, Yasmin, was sitting alone under a tree. She looked a bit sad.

Aliyah wanted to keep playing on the swings, but she remembered what her mother had said about being a good friend. She decided to go over and see what was wrong. "Yasmin, are you okay?" she asked gently.

Yasmin looked up and sighed, "I forgot my lunch at home. I'm hungry and don't know what to do." Aliyah felt a pang of sympathy. She had her favorite sandwich, but Yasmin didn't have anything to eat.

Aliyah thought for a moment. She could ignore it and keep playing, but that wouldn't be very kind. She remembered the importance of **'Ukhuwwah'**, which means brotherhood and friendship in Islam. It means helping your friends and being there for them when they need you.

Aliyah smiled and said, "Don't worry, Yasmin! I'll share my lunch with you." Yasmin's face brightened, and she said, "Really? Thank you, Aliyah!"

Aliyah ran back to her bag, took out her sandwich and juice, and sat down next to Yasmin. She shared her sandwich with Yasmin. They shared the juice and started talking and laughing together. Yasmin seemed much happier now.

After lunch, the teacher organized a three-legged race. Aliyah and Yasmin teamed up. At first, they had trouble coordinating their steps, and they kept stumbling. Aliyah was eager to win, but she noticed that Yasmin was getting frustrated.

Instead of rushing ahead, Aliyah slowed down and said, "Let's go slowly and try to match our steps." Yasmin nodded, and they began to work together, moving carefully but steadily. They didn't win the race, but they finished it with big smiles on their faces, feeling proud of their teamwork.

Later, while they were sitting on the grass, Yasmin said, "Thank you, Aliyah. You're a true friend. You made me feel better today." Aliyah felt a warm feeling inside. She realized that friendship, or Ukhuwwah, wasn't about winning races or having the best lunch. It was about being there for each other, listening, and sharing.

At the end of the day, Aliyah noticed Sara, her other friend, was looking upset because she lost her favorite toy. Aliyah quickly went over to help her search for it. After a while, they found the toy under a bench, and Sara hugged Aliyah, saying, "You're always such a great friend!"

Aliyah smiled, feeling happy and proud. She understood that being a good friend meant caring, sharing, and helping, not just having fun together. She decided that she would always practice Ukhuwwah, knowing it made everyone feel loved and valued.

Moral of the Story: Being a good friend means listening, being kind, and helping others whenever they need it.

Chapter 23

Respecting Personal Space: A Story of Boundaries – Hudud

Adam loved playing with his friends at school. One day, during art class, he saw his friend Bilal drawing a beautiful picture. Curious, Adam leaned over Bilal's shoulder and started asking questions. "What are you drawing? Can I see? Why are you using that color?" he asked, getting closer and closer.

Bilal felt uncomfortable and couldn't focus on his drawing. He tried to move his paper away, but Adam kept leaning in. "Adam, you're too close!" Bilal finally said, sounding a little annoyed. Adam frowned, feeling confused. He didn't understand why Bilal seemed upset.

Later, during recess, Adam noticed his friend Maryam writing in her diary under a tree. He quickly ran over and tried to peek into her diary. "What are you writing, Maryam?" he asked, leaning in. Maryam quickly closed her diary and said, "That's private, Adam! You shouldn't look!"

Adam felt surprised. He thought he was just being friendly and curious, but Maryam looked upset. She moved away and sat somewhere else. Adam felt bad and didn't understand why his friends were reacting this way.

That afternoon, Adam's teacher, Miss Leila, gathered the class and explained, "Today, we are going to talk about '**Hudud**', which means respecting boundaries in Islam. Everyone has personal space and privacy that we must respect. It's important to ask for permission before entering someone's space or looking at something private."

Adam listened carefully and started to understand. He realized he had crossed his friends' boundaries by getting too close and peeking into their private things without asking. He felt a little embarrassed but decided to make things right.

The next day, during art class, Adam saw Bilal drawing again. This time, he stood at a distance and asked, "Bilal, may I see your drawing?" Bilal smiled and nodded, "Sure, come and see." Adam walked over and stood beside him, giving him enough space. Bilal showed him the picture, and they both talked happily about the colors and shapes.

During recess, Adam saw Maryam sitting under the tree again with her diary. He remembered what Miss Leila had taught them. He walked over and said, "Hi, Maryam! I'm sorry for trying to peek into your diary yesterday. I understand it's private."

Maryam smiled, feeling happy that Adam understood. "Thank you, Adam. I appreciate it," she replied. They started talking about other fun things, and Maryam seemed much more comfortable.

Later, while playing a game, Adam noticed another friend, Ahmed, seemed bothered whenever someone stood too close. Remembering what he had learned, Adam asked, "Ahmed, is this too close? Should I move back?" Ahmed nodded and said, "Yes, thank you, Adam!" and smiled.

Adam realized that respecting personal space, or Hudud, made everyone feel comfortable and happy. It wasn't just about being polite but about caring for his friends' feelings too.

From that day on, Adam always remembered to give his friends space and privacy, knowing it showed respect and kindness.

Moral of the Story: Respect others' personal space and privacy to make them feel comfortable and valued.

Chapter 24

Thank You for Your Hard Work: Appreciating Others - Shukr

Salma was always busy playing with her toys, reading her favorite books, and running around with her friends. One morning, she woke up late and found her breakfast already on the table. She ate quickly and rushed to school, without thinking about who had made her breakfast or cleaned her room.

At school, Salma had a fun day learning and playing. Her teacher, Miss Hana, taught the class a new song. Salma enjoyed it so much, but she didn't think to thank Miss Hana for teaching it to her. After school, she grabbed her backpack and ran out to play with her friends, leaving her books and papers scattered all over her desk.

That evening, Salma was looking for her favorite red dress to wear, but she couldn't find it anywhere. She went to her mother and asked, "Mom, where is my red dress?"

Her mother replied, "I just finished washing it and hung it up to dry. You'll have to wear something else today."

Salma felt annoyed and stomped her foot. "But I wanted to wear it now!" she complained. Her mother looked tired and didn't say anything.

Later, at dinner, Salma noticed her father looked tired too. He had been working all day. He smiled and asked Salma, "How was your day, sweetie?" Salma chatted away happily but didn't notice how tired her father looked.

The next day, Miss Hana asked the class to write a story about someone they were thankful for. Salma scratched her head, trying to think of someone. She realized she didn't say "thank you" very often.

During recess, Salma saw the janitor, Mr. Karim, sweeping the floors and cleaning up after the children. She noticed he looked tired but kept working hard with a smile on his face. Salma suddenly felt bad for never saying thank you to him.

After school, Salma decided to talk to her parents. She said, "Mom, Dad, I just realized I haven't been very thankful. I never thanked you for making my meals or washing my clothes." Her parents smiled warmly, and her mother replied, "That's okay, Salma. It's important to learn to say 'thank you,' or **'Shukr'**, for all the things people do for us."

Salma felt a little ashamed but also determined to do better. The next morning, she woke up early and made her bed. She went to the kitchen and said, "Thank you for making my breakfast, Mom!" Her mother smiled brightly, "You're welcome, Salma!"

At school, Salma went to Miss Hana and said, "Thank you for teaching us the new song yesterday. It was so much fun!" Miss Hana's face lit up with a big smile, "Thank you for saying that, Salma!"

During recess, Salma went to Mr. Karim and said, "Thank you for keeping our school clean, Mr. Karim!" He was surprised but very happy and said, "Thank you, Salma. That means a lot to me."

By the end of the day, Salma felt much happier. She realized that showing appreciation, or Shukr, made others feel good and brought joy to her heart too.

Moral of the Story: Always say thank you and show appreciation for the hard work others do to make your life better.

Chapter 25

The Truth Always Wins: Speaking the Truth - Haqq

Hassan was playing in the living room with his favorite toy car. He loved to race it around, making zooming noises as it sped across the floor. His mother had told him to play carefully because there was a glass vase on the table nearby.

As Hassan was racing his car, it suddenly slipped out of his hand, hit the table, and the vase fell to the floor with a loud crash. The glass shattered into pieces. Hassan's eyes widened in fear. He knew his mother would be upset.

He quickly thought, "What should I do? Should I tell the truth or say it wasn't me?" Just then, his mother walked into the room and saw the broken vase. She asked, "Hassan, what happened here?"

Hassan felt his heart pounding. He thought about lying and saying he didn't know, but then he remembered what his father had taught him about '**Haqq**', which means speaking the truth in Islam. His father had always said that telling the truth was the right thing to do, even when it was hard.

Hassan took a deep breath and decided to be honest. He looked at his mother and said, "I'm sorry, Mama. I was playing with my toy car, and it hit the table. I didn't mean to break the vase."

His mother sighed but then smiled gently. "Thank you for telling me the truth, Hassan," she said. "I'm not happy that the vase is broken, but I'm proud of you for being honest. That's very important."

Hassan felt relieved. He knew he had done the right thing by telling the truth.

Later that day, Hassan was at school, playing with his friend Amir. They were running around when Amir tripped and fell, tearing his pants. The teacher, Miss Nadia, asked, "What happened, Amir?"

Amir looked nervous and didn't know what to say. Hassan knew it was an accident, but he also knew Amir might get into trouble. He thought about staying quiet, but he remembered Haqq and how important it was to speak the truth.

Hassan raised his hand and said, "Miss Nadia, it wasn't Amir's fault. We were both running, and it was an accident. I'm sorry if we were running too fast."

Miss Nadia nodded and said, "Thank you for being honest, Hassan. Remember, running inside can be dangerous, but I'm glad you told the truth."

Amir smiled at Hassan and whispered, "Thanks for telling the truth. You're a good friend."

That afternoon, Hassan went home feeling happy. He realized that speaking the truth, or practicing Haqq, made him feel good inside and helped his friends too. He promised himself that he would always try to be honest, even when it wasn't easy.

Later, when his father came home, Hassan told him what had happened. His father smiled proudly and said, "Hassan, you did the right thing. Telling the truth shows courage and makes people trust you more."

Hassan felt proud. He learned that speaking the truth was always the best choice, no matter what. It made everyone feel better and brought peace to his heart.

Moral of the Story: Always tell the truth, even when it is hard, because honesty builds trust and makes everyone feel happy and safe.

Chapter 26

Helping Hands at Home: A Story of Responsibility - Masooliyyah

Amina loved playing with her dolls and drawing pictures, but she didn't enjoy doing chores at home. One Saturday morning, Amina woke up to see her mother cleaning the kitchen and her father mowing the lawn. Her little brother was picking up his toys in the living room.

Amina wanted to play with her toys, so she quietly sneaked past her family and went to her room. She thought, "I don't feel like doing chores today." She began to color a picture, but soon she heard her mother call, "Amina, could you help me with the dishes?"

Amina frowned and muttered, "I don't want to." She pretended not to hear and continued coloring. A few minutes later, her father called, "Amina, can you help me with the groceries?"

Again, Amina didn't want to stop playing, so she ignored him too. Soon, her little brother came in and asked, "Amina, can you help me find my lost toy?" Amina replied, "I'm busy. Find it yourself."

As the day went on, Amina noticed that her mother looked tired from cooking and cleaning all morning. Her father seemed exhausted after working in the garden. Her brother was sad because he couldn't find his toy. Amina began to feel a little guilty.

Later, Amina's grandmother came to visit. She saw everyone looking tired and asked, "What's wrong?" Amina's mother explained, "We've been working all morning, but Amina hasn't been helping us."

Amina's grandmother smiled gently and said, "Amina, in our home, everyone has a role to play. Helping each other is part of our '**Masooliyyah**', our responsibility. It makes the work easier for everyone and keeps the home happy."

Amina listened carefully and realized she had not been doing her part. She felt ashamed but decided to make things right. She got up and went to her mother and said, "I'm sorry, Mom. I will help with the dishes now."

Her mother smiled warmly, "Thank you, Amina." Amina washed the dishes while her mother dried them. Then, she went to her father and offered to help him with the groceries. "I'm here to help now, Dad," she said.

Her father looked surprised but happy. "Thank you, Amina," he said. They carried the groceries together and put them away in the kitchen. After that, Amina went to her brother and said, "Let's find your toy together!" They searched under the couch and behind the curtains until they finally found the lost toy.

Her brother jumped with joy and hugged Amina. "Thank you, Amina! You're the best!" he exclaimed.

By the end of the day, everyone seemed happier. Amina felt proud of herself for helping her family. She realized that helping with chores was not just work; it was a way to show love and care for her family. She learned that her role, or Masooliyyah, was important in keeping her home a happy place.

From that day on, Amina made sure to help with the chores, knowing that every little bit of help made a big difference.

Moral of the Story: Helping at home is a responsibility that shows love and care for your family, and it makes everyone feel happy and appreciated.

Chapter 27

Modesty in Dress: A Lesson in Islamic Attire - Haya

Yara loved dressing up in bright colors and fancy clothes. One day, her mother took her shopping for new clothes. Yara picked out a sparkly dress with short sleeves and a shiny skirt. She twirled around in front of the mirror and said, "I love this dress! Can I wear it to the park?"

Her mother smiled and said, "It's very pretty, Yara, but remember, we also need to think about modesty, or **Haya**, when we choose what to wear."

Yara frowned a little, not sure what her mother meant. "What is Haya?" she asked. Her mother explained, "Haya means modesty in Islam. It's about dressing in a way that shows respect for ourselves and others, keeping in mind that our clothes should cover us properly."

Yara listened and thought for a moment. She didn't fully understand but nodded anyway. Her mother then picked out a dress with long sleeves and a matching scarf. It was still colorful and pretty but more modest. "Why don't you try this one, Yara?" she suggested.

Yara tried on the new dress and looked at herself in the mirror. It was different from what she usually wore, but she liked the way it felt—comfortable and beautiful in a simple way.

The next day, Yara wore her new dress to school. Her friends noticed and said, "That dress is nice, Yara!" She felt proud and happy.

Later, during recess, Yara saw her friend Leena playing on the swings. Leena was wearing a very short skirt, and when she swung high, her skirt flew up, and she looked embarrassed. Yara realized that modest clothes could help her feel more comfortable and safe while playing.

After school, Yara went to the park with her family. She saw some kids running around, and one of them fell and hurt their knee. Yara ran over to help and noticed that her modest dress allowed her to move around easily without worrying about her clothes.

That evening, Yara's grandmother came to visit. Yara proudly showed her new dress and said, "Look, Grandma, I chose a dress that is modest!" Her grandmother smiled and hugged her. "That's wonderful, Yara. Remember, modesty is not just about clothes; it's also about how we behave and treat others."

Yara nodded, understanding a bit more about **'Haya'**. The next day, at school, Yara noticed a new girl in her class who seemed shy and quiet. She decided to be friendly and said, "Hi! My name is Yara. Would you like to play with us?"

The new girl smiled and joined in. Yara realized that being modest wasn't just about wearing the right clothes; it was also about being kind and respectful to others.

From then on, Yara always thought carefully about what she wore and how she acted. She understood that Haya, or modesty, was about showing respect for herself and everyone around her.

Moral of the Story: Modesty in dress and actions shows respect for ourselves and others, making everyone feel comfortable and valued.

Chapter 28

Listening with Care: The Value of Attention - Insat

Ibrahim loved to talk. He enjoyed sharing stories about his day, telling jokes, and chatting with his friends. But when others spoke, he often found himself daydreaming or thinking about what he wanted to say next. He didn't always pay attention.

One day, during story time at school, Miss Sara, his teacher, was reading a new story about a brave lion. Ibrahim was excited at first, but soon he started fidgeting and looking out the window. He didn't listen to the end of the story and missed the part about how the lion saved his friends.

When Miss Sara asked, "What did the lion do to help his friends?" Ibrahim had no idea. His classmates raised their hands eagerly, but Ibrahim felt embarrassed. He realized he hadn't been listening.

Later, during lunch, Ibrahim was talking to his friend Ali about his favorite cartoon. Ali tried to tell him about a new game he had learned, but Ibrahim kept interrupting with his own stories. Ali looked a little annoyed and walked away.

That evening, at home, Ibrahim's mother was giving him instructions on how to help set the table for dinner. She asked him to bring the plates, forks, and glasses. But Ibrahim was busy thinking about his toys and only half-listened. He brought the plates but forgot the forks and glasses.

His mother sighed, "Ibrahim, you need to listen carefully. I asked for plates, forks, and glasses." Ibrahim felt guilty and realized that he hadn't been paying attention.

The next day, Miss Sara talked to the class about **'Insat'**, which means listening with attention in Islam. She explained, "Listening carefully shows respect. It helps us understand others and makes them feel valued."

Ibrahim thought about what his teacher said. He realized that he hadn't been showing respect by not listening to his friends, teachers, or even his parents.

That afternoon, Ibrahim decided to do better. During story time, he sat up straight and listened carefully to Miss Sara. He heard every word and learned how the lion saved his friends by being brave and smart. When Miss Sara asked, "What did the lion do?" Ibrahim raised his hand confidently and answered correctly. Miss Sara smiled and said, "Good job, Ibrahim! You were listening very well today."

At lunchtime, Ibrahim asked Ali, "Can you tell me more about that new game?" This time, he stayed quiet and listened carefully as Ali explained the rules. Ali smiled and said, "Thanks for listening, Ibrahim. Let's play it together!" They both laughed and had fun playing the new game.

Later, at home, Ibrahim's father was teaching him how to tie his shoelaces. Ibrahim listened carefully, watching his father's hands and following his instructions step by step. He tried and tried, and finally, he did it! His father patted him on the back and said, "Good job, Ibrahim! You learned because you listened well."

Ibrahim felt proud. He realized that listening with care, or Insat, made everything better. It showed respect and helped him learn and understand.

From that day on, Ibrahim made sure to listen carefully to his parents, teachers, and friends, knowing it was an important way to show respect and learn new things.

Moral of the Story: Listening carefully shows respect and helps us learn, understand, and connect with others.

Chapter 29

Kind Words to Animals: A Lesson in Mercy - Rifq

Adam loved going to the park with his friends after school. One sunny afternoon, as they were playing, Adam noticed a stray cat sitting near the bushes. The cat was small and had a fluffy tail. It looked hungry and tired, its fur a bit dirty. Some of the kids started throwing little stones at the cat, laughing as it tried to run away.

Adam picked up a small pebble too, thinking it would be fun, but he paused. The cat's eyes looked scared, and it huddled close to the ground. Adam felt a little strange inside. He remembered what his mother had said about being kind to all of Allah's creatures.

Adam dropped the pebble and walked over to his friends, saying, "Hey, let's not throw stones at the cat. It looks scared." The other kids stopped and looked at him. "Why not?" one of them asked. Adam replied, "Because it's not right to hurt animals. They are Allah's creatures too, and we should treat them with kindness, or **'Rifq'**."

Some of the kids shrugged and went back to playing, but Adam felt he should do something more. He went home, grabbed a bowl, and filled it with milk. He returned to the park and slowly approached the cat, speaking softly, "It's okay, little cat. I won't hurt you."

The cat was still wary, but it could smell the milk. Adam placed the bowl gently on the ground and stepped back. The cat slowly came closer, sniffing the air. Finally, it lapped up the milk, its little pink tongue moving quickly.

Adam smiled, feeling happy that the cat was eating. He sat quietly, watching the cat enjoy the milk. After it finished, the cat looked up and meowed softly, as if saying thank you. Adam felt warm inside and knew he had done the right thing.

The next day, Adam saw a group of boys chasing pigeons in the park. They were running around, trying to scare the birds. Adam remembered his lesson from the day before and said, "Stop chasing the pigeons! They are just trying to find food and rest."

The boys stopped and asked, "Why should we care?" Adam replied, "Because we must show mercy, or Rifq, to all of Allah's creatures. The Prophet Muhammad (peace be upon him) taught us to be kind to animals and never harm them."

The boys listened, and some nodded. They realized that Adam was right. They all decided to sit down and watch the pigeons peacefully. Adam took out some bread crumbs from his pocket and gently scattered them on the ground. The pigeons, seeing there was no more danger, came back and started eating.

Adam felt proud that he had spread kindness to his friends too. He realized that showing mercy to animals was just as important as being kind to people. Later that evening, his father saw him feeding the stray cat again and said, "I'm proud of you, Adam. You are showing true Rifq, mercy, to Allah's creatures."

Adam knew he would always remember to treat animals with care and kindness. He felt happy knowing that small acts of mercy made a big difference.

Moral of the Story: Always treat animals with kindness and care because they are Allah's creatures, and they deserve our mercy and respect.

Chapter 30

The Power of Dua: Always Asking Allah - Dua

Hana was excited about the school play. She had been practicing her lines for weeks and wanted to do her best. But the day before the play, she felt a scratch in her throat. By the evening, she had a sore throat and started coughing. Hana grew worried. "Oh no, what if I can't speak tomorrow?" she thought.

Her mother noticed and said, "Hana, don't worry. Have you made a **'Dua'** to ask Allah for help?" Hana looked up, surprised. "But will Allah really listen to me?" she asked. Her mother smiled gently and replied, "Of course, Hana! Allah always listens to our Duas. We can ask for anything, big or small."

That night, before going to bed, Hana raised her hands and whispered a Dua, "Dear Allah, please help me feel better so I can speak in the play tomorrow." She felt a little calmer and fell asleep.

The next morning, Hana woke up feeling a bit better, but her voice was still soft. She felt worried again, but she remembered her Dua. At breakfast, she made another Dua, "Dear Allah, please make my voice strong for the play." She drank some warm water and honey, just like her mother suggested.

At school, Hana's teacher noticed she was quiet and asked, "Are you okay, Hana?" Hana explained about her sore throat. Her teacher smiled and said, "Remember, Hana, always make Dua and trust Allah. Everything will be okay."

Before the play began, Hana felt nervous. She whispered another Dua, "Dear Allah, please help me do my best." As she stepped onto the stage, her heart was pounding, but she felt a sudden sense of calm. When it was her turn to speak, her voice came out clearer and stronger than she had expected. She spoke all her lines perfectly, and everyone clapped.

After the play, Hana's friends said, "Wow, Hana! You did great!" Hana felt so happy and thankful. She realized that her Duas had been answered.

That evening, Hana thought about what happened. She realized that making Dua wasn't just for big things, but also for everyday needs. She decided to make Dua more often.

The next day, Hana lost her favorite pencil at school. She searched everywhere but couldn't find it. She felt sad but then remembered, "I can make a Dua." She quietly asked, "Dear Allah, please help me find my pencil."

A few minutes later, her friend Sara came over and said, "Hana, I found a pencil under the desk. Is this yours?" Hana smiled brightly and said, "Yes! Thank you, Sara!" She felt thankful to Allah for answering her Dua so quickly.

From then on, Hana made a habit of making Dua every day, whether for big things or small. She knew that Allah was always listening, ready to help.

Moral of the Story: Always make Dua to Allah for everything, trusting that Allah listens to every prayer, no matter how big or small.

Chapter 31

Standing Up for Justice: A Brave Little Girl - Qist

Aisha was excited about the school's art competition. She had worked very hard on her drawing of a beautiful garden with colorful flowers, birds, and butterflies. She had used all her favorite colors and had spent many days making sure every detail was perfect.

On the day of the competition, all the students brought their drawings to the classroom. The teacher, Miss Nadia, displayed them on a board. Aisha proudly put her drawing up, and everyone admired it. "Wow, Aisha, your garden is so pretty!" her friend Maryam said.

Later, while Aisha was playing outside during recess, she saw her classmate, Rania, standing nervously by the board. Rania's drawing was placed right next to Aisha's, but it was much simpler, with only a few flowers and no bright colors. Aisha heard some kids giggling behind Rania, whispering, "Her drawing looks so plain next to Aisha's. She'll never win."

Aisha noticed that Rania looked sad and worried. She remembered her parents teaching her about '**Qist'**, which means justice in Islam. It means treating everyone fairly, no matter what. Aisha knew it wasn't fair to make fun of Rania just because her drawing was different.

After recess, Aisha saw Rania quietly moving her drawing to the back of the board, hiding it behind others. Aisha felt a pang in her heart.

She walked over to Rania and gently said, "Rania, why are you moving your drawing?"

Rania sighed and said, "My drawing isn't as good as yours, Aisha. Everyone is laughing at it."

Aisha felt sad for Rania. She realized she needed to stand up for what was right. She called her friends and said, "It's not fair to make fun of someone's work. Everyone has their own style, and every drawing is special. Let's put Rania's drawing back up where it belongs."

Her friends nodded and helped Aisha move Rania's drawing back to the front. Then, Aisha said loudly, "I think Rania's drawing is beautiful because it has her own special touch. We should appreciate everyone's efforts."

The other kids stopped giggling and looked thoughtful. Some nodded in agreement, realizing they had been unfair.

The next day, Miss Nadia announced the winners of the art competition. She said, "This year, we have two special awards. One for creativity and one for fairness. The creativity award goes to Aisha for her beautiful garden drawing. And the fairness award goes to Rania, for her lovely simple design and for bravely showing her work."

Everyone clapped, and Rania's face lit up with a big smile. She looked at Aisha and said, "Thank you, Aisha, for standing up for me."

Aisha smiled back, feeling proud. She knew she had done the right thing by practicing Qist — standing up for justice and treating everyone fairly. She learned that fairness wasn't just about winning, but also about making sure everyone felt included and respected.

Moral of the Story: Always treat everyone fairly and stand up for what is right, because fairness brings happiness and kindness to everyone.

Chapter 32

Using Time Wisely: The Story of Productivity - Barakah

USING TIME WISELY: THE STORY OF PRODUCTIVITY - BARAKAH

Omar loved playing games on his tablet. Every day after school, he would come home, drop his bag, and start playing. One afternoon, his mother reminded him, "Omar, you have homework to do." But Omar thought, "I'll do it later," and continued playing his game.

An hour passed, and then another. By the time Omar decided to start his homework, it was already late, and he was feeling tired. He rushed through his work, making mistakes and feeling frustrated. The next day, his teacher said, "Omar, you didn't do your homework properly. You need to be more careful next time."

Omar felt sad and realized that he should have started his homework earlier. He didn't like feeling rushed and knew he could do better.

The next day, Omar's father talked to him and said, "Omar, time is a blessing, or **'Barakah'**. When we use our time wisely, we can get more done and feel happier. Let's think of a way to manage your time better."

Omar listened carefully and thought about what his father said. He decided to make a plan. After school, he would spend some time doing his homework first, then play games as a reward. He set a timer for 30 minutes to start.

The next afternoon, Omar came home and, instead of grabbing his tablet, he opened his homework book. He worked carefully and finished his homework on time. He felt proud because he knew he did a good job. After that, he played his favorite game, feeling happy and relaxed because his work was already done.

Omar noticed that by using his time wisely, he had more time to do the things he enjoyed. He realized that he felt less stressed and more relaxed. The next day, he even had extra time to help his mother in the kitchen, and she smiled and said, "Thank you, Omar. You're being very helpful today!"

Later, at school, his teacher praised him, "Good job on your homework, Omar! You did it neatly and carefully." Omar felt proud and realized that using time wisely was helping him do better in everything.

One day, Omar's friend Ali was worried because he had a big project due, but he hadn't started yet. He asked Omar, "How do you get your homework done so quickly now?"

Omar replied, "I learned that time is a blessing, Barakah. I make a plan, do my work first, and then have time to play. It makes everything easier!"

Ali decided to try Omar's way, and soon, he also found himself finishing his work on time and enjoying his playtime more. They both felt happier and more relaxed.

From that day on, Omar always remembered that time was a precious gift. He learned that making the best use of every moment helped him do better in school and enjoy his free time.

Moral of the Story: Use your time wisely because time is a blessing, and managing it well helps you do better and feel happier.

Chapter 33

Respecting Others' Beliefs: A Story of Tolerance - Tasamuh

Zayd loved his school and his friends. One day, a new boy named Arjun joined his class. Arjun had just moved to their town, and he came from a different country. On his first day, Zayd noticed that Arjun wore a small necklace with a symbol he had never seen before. During lunch, Arjun sat alone, looking shy.

Zayd wanted to be friendly, so he invited Arjun to sit with him and his friends. As they ate, Zayd asked, "What is that necklace you're wearing?" Arjun smiled and said, "It's a symbol from my religion. It's very special to me." Zayd nodded but didn't say much.

Later during playtime, some of Zayd's friends whispered, "Arjun is different. He prays differently and has strange customs." They started giggling and pointing at Arjun's necklace. Zayd felt a bit unsure. He liked Arjun but didn't know much about his culture or beliefs.

The next day, Zayd noticed that Arjun was again sitting by himself during lunch. He felt sad for Arjun and remembered what his teacher had told them about '**Tasamuh**', which means tolerance in Islam. It means respecting everyone, no matter what their beliefs or customs are.

Zayd decided to sit next to Arjun and said, "Can you tell me more about your necklace and your religion?" Arjun's face brightened, and he explained, "This symbol represents peace and goodness in my faith. We believe in being kind to everyone."

Zayd listened carefully and realized that even though Arjun's beliefs were different, they shared the same values of kindness and peace. Zayd smiled and said, "That's really interesting, Arjun. I think it's cool to learn about new things."

That afternoon, their teacher, Miss Layla, gave a lesson about different cultures and religions. She explained how people around the world have different ways of praying, eating, and celebrating, but all these differences make the world a more colorful place. "This is called Tasamuh, respecting and appreciating everyone's beliefs and traditions," she said.

Zayd felt proud to have asked Arjun about his necklace. He realized that learning about others made them closer friends. At recess, he invited Arjun to join a game of soccer. As they played, Zayd's friends noticed how friendly Arjun was and started to include him in their games too.

Over time, Zayd and Arjun became good friends. Zayd also learned about other cultures and customs. One day, Zayd saw another new student, Maria, who was wearing a different kind of headscarf. Zayd smiled and remembered Tasamuh. He went over and said, "Hi, Maria! Welcome to our school. Would you like to join us?"

Maria smiled back and nodded. Zayd felt happy knowing that he was practicing Tasamuh, showing respect and kindness to everyone, no matter where they came from or what they believed.

From that day on, Zayd always remembered the importance of respecting others' beliefs. He knew that Tasamuh made their school a happier and more welcoming place for everyone.

Moral of the Story: Respect everyone's beliefs and traditions because it brings peace, kindness, and understanding to the world.

Chapter 34

The Golden Rule: Treating Others as You Want to Be Treated - Ma'ruf

Mariam was excited to go to school because today was "Show and Tell" day. She had brought her favorite teddy bear, Mr. Fuzzy, and couldn't wait to show it to her friends. She held Mr. Fuzzy tightly, feeling happy and proud.

When it was time for Show and Tell, Mariam went to the front of the class and said, "This is Mr. Fuzzy. He is my best friend, and I take him everywhere!" The class clapped, and Mariam felt proud. She handed Mr. Fuzzy to her friend, Samira, so everyone could have a closer look.

But then, as Mr. Fuzzy went around the class, a boy named Ahmed pulled on one of Mr. Fuzzy's ears too hard, and it tore a little. Mariam gasped and quickly ran over. "Please be gentle! Mr. Fuzzy is special to me," she said with tears in her eyes.

Ahmed felt a little bad but shrugged and said, "It's just a teddy bear." Mariam felt upset. She didn't like how Ahmed had treated her favorite toy.

The next day, Ahmed brought his new toy car to school. It was shiny and blue, and he proudly showed it to everyone. Mariam remembered how Ahmed had treated Mr. Fuzzy and felt a bit angry. When the toy car came to her, she thought about pulling off one of its wheels.

But then, she remembered what her mother had taught her about **'Ma'ruf'**, which means treating others as you want to be treated. She realized that if she broke Ahmed's toy, she would be just as unkind as he had been. Mariam decided to be gentle and handed the car back carefully, smiling.

Later during recess, Ahmed came over to Mariam and said, "I'm sorry, Mariam. I didn't mean to hurt Mr. Fuzzy. I was just playing too roughly." Mariam smiled and said, "It's okay, Ahmed. I understand. But remember, we should always treat others and their things the way we want to be treated."

Ahmed nodded, understanding now. He felt happy that Mariam had been kind to his toy car, even though he hadn't been careful with her teddy bear. "Thank you for not breaking my toy car," he said. "I'll be more careful next time."

After that, they played together and shared their toys with each other. They laughed and had fun, treating each other with kindness and respect. Mariam felt good knowing she had chosen the right thing to do.

The next day, the teacher noticed how nicely Mariam and Ahmed were playing. She said, "I'm proud of both of you for practicing Ma'ruf.

Treating others the way you want to be treated makes everyone feel happy and respected."

From then on, both Mariam and Ahmed always remembered the lesson of Ma'ruf. They knew that treating others kindly would bring more kindness and happiness to everyone.

Moral of the Story: Always treat others the way you want to be treated, with kindness and respect, because it makes everyone feel happy and valued.

Chapter 35

Control Your Anger: The Power of Calm - Hilm

Leila loved to play with her friends, but sometimes, when things didn't go her way, she felt her face getting hot, and her fists tightening. She got angry quickly, like when her friend Ali accidentally knocked over her blocks, or when her little sister borrowed her favorite crayon without asking.

One day at school, Leila was playing a game of tag. She was about to catch her friend Fatima when another boy, Omar, bumped into her. Leila stumbled and fell. She felt her anger bubbling up like a volcano. "Omar, why did you do that?" she shouted, her face turning red.

Omar looked surprised. "I didn't mean to, Leila," he said quietly. But Leila was too angry to listen. She crossed her arms and stomped away, feeling upset.

At home, her mother noticed that Leila was quiet and asked, "Leila, is everything okay?" Leila told her about what happened at school. Her mother smiled gently and said, "Leila, I understand that you felt angry, but do you know about '**Hilm**'?"

Leila shook her head. Her mother continued, "Hilm means controlling your anger and staying calm. When we feel angry, there are things we can do to help ourselves calm down."

Leila was curious. "What can I do, Mama?" she asked.

Her mother replied, "First, take a deep breath. Breathe in slowly through your nose and out through your mouth. It helps cool down the fire inside. Then, count to ten in your head. If you still feel angry, find a quiet place to sit and calm down."

Leila thought about this and decided to try it the next time she felt angry.

The next day, at school, Leila was playing with her friend Sara. They were drawing pictures together, but when Leila reached for the blue crayon, Sara grabbed it first. Leila felt her anger rising again. Her face felt hot, and she wanted to shout.

But then, she remembered what her mother had said. Leila stopped, took a deep breath in through her nose, and slowly let it out through her mouth. She counted to ten in her head. Slowly, she felt herself starting to calm down.

She said to Sara in a gentle voice, "Could I please have the blue crayon when you're done?" Sara smiled and replied, "Of course, Leila! I'll be done soon." Leila felt proud of herself for staying calm. She realized that controlling her anger made her feel better and helped her friends feel happy too.

Later that day, during story time, Omar came over and said, "Leila, I'm really sorry about yesterday. I didn't mean to bump into you." Leila smiled and said, "It's okay, Omar. I was angry, but I'm learning to control it. Let's play together today!"

Omar grinned, and they joined their friends in a game. Leila felt peaceful inside. She understood that practicing Hilm, controlling her anger, helped her feel happier and made her friendships stronger.

From that day on, Leila always remembered to take a deep breath and count to ten whenever she felt angry. She knew that staying calm brought peace and happiness to everyone around her.

Moral of the Story: Controlling your anger and staying calm helps everyone feel happy and brings peace to your heart.

Chapter 36

Use Your Ears First: The Lesson of Listening – Sama'

Bilal loved to talk. He always had a story to share or a joke to tell. During class, he would often raise his hand, eager to answer questions before anyone else. But sometimes, he was so busy thinking about what he wanted to say that he didn't listen carefully to what others were saying.

One day, during science class, the teacher, Miss Amina, asked, "What is the most important thing plants need to grow?" Bilal quickly raised his hand and shouted, "Water!" Miss Amina nodded and said, "That's correct, but there are other things too. Can anyone else add to that?"

Before she could finish, Bilal jumped in again, saying, "Sunlight!" Miss Amina smiled and replied, "Yes, that's true. But let's hear from someone else, Bilal."

Bilal felt a bit embarrassed. He realized he had spoken out of turn without listening carefully.

Later, during break time, Bilal's friend, Yusuf, came over with a big smile. "Bilal, I have a great idea for our school project!" he started. But before Yusuf could explain, Bilal interrupted, "I know! Let's make a volcano that erupts!"

Yusuf looked disappointed and said, "Actually, I was thinking of something different." Bilal realized he hadn't listened to Yusuf's idea at all. Yusuf walked away to play with someone else, and Bilal felt bad.

That evening, at home, Bilal's mother noticed that he seemed quiet. She asked, "What's wrong, Bilal?" He told her about what happened in class and with Yusuf. His mother smiled and said, "Bilal, in Islam, we have a special word for listening carefully. It's called '**Sama''**. It means to use your ears first before you speak. Listening is a sign of wisdom."

Bilal thought about this and decided to practice Sama' the next day.

The following day at school, Miss Amina asked another question, "Can anyone tell me what animals need to survive?" Bilal was excited, but he remembered his mother's advice. He took a deep breath and waited.

His friend Fatima raised her hand and said, "Animals need food and water." Miss Amina nodded and added, "That's right, and what else?" Bilal listened carefully. Another classmate added, "They also need shelter."

When it was finally Bilal's turn to speak, he said, "And they need space to live and grow." Miss Amina smiled widely, "Excellent answer, Bilal! I'm glad you listened first."

Bilal felt proud and realized that he had learned something new by listening to others.

During recess, Yusuf approached Bilal again. This time, Bilal said, "Tell me about your idea for the project, Yusuf." Yusuf smiled and shared his plan for making a solar system model. Bilal listened carefully and then said, "That's a great idea! Let's work on it together!"

Yusuf was happy, and they both started planning the project with excitement. Bilal felt good knowing he had practiced Sama' by listening first.

From then on, Bilal always remembered to use his ears first and listen carefully before speaking. He knew that listening made him wiser and helped him learn more from others.

Moral of the Story: Always listen first before speaking, as listening carefully shows wisdom and respect for others.

Chapter 37

Guard Your Tongue: Think Before You Speak - Hifz al-Lisan

Maryam loved talking to her friends at school. She was always full of stories and jokes. But sometimes, without thinking, she would say things that made others feel upset or sad.

One day, during art class, Maryam's friend Noor was showing her drawing of a butterfly. Maryam glanced at the drawing and giggled, "That doesn't look like a butterfly! It looks more like a scribble!" Noor's smile disappeared, and her eyes filled with tears. She quickly covered her drawing with her hands and turned away.

Maryam felt a little bad, but she thought, "I was just being honest." Later that day, she overheard her friends, Sara and Amina, whispering. Curious, she walked over and said loudly, "What are you two whispering about? Are you keeping secrets?"

Sara looked uncomfortable and replied, "We're just talking about something private." Maryam shrugged and said, "Secrets are silly. You should tell everyone!" Amina frowned, and both girls walked away, feeling upset.

That evening, Maryam's mother noticed that Maryam looked unhappy and asked, "Maryam, is something bothering you?" Maryam explained what happened with Noor, Sara, and Amina. Her mother listened and said, "Maryam, do you know about '**Hifz al-Lisan**'?"

Maryam shook her head. Her mother continued, "Hifz al-Lisan means guarding your tongue. It's about thinking before you speak and choosing words that are kind and thoughtful. Our words have power. They can either hurt or heal."

Maryam thought about what her mother said and realized she hadn't been careful with her words. She decided to try and do better the next day.

The following morning, during break time, Maryam saw Noor sitting alone with her drawing. She remembered her mother's words about guarding her tongue. She walked over gently and said, "Noor, I'm sorry for what I said yesterday. Your butterfly is very colorful and creative. Can you show me how you made it?"

Noor looked up, surprised, but then she smiled. "Thank you, Maryam," she said softly, and they spent the rest of the break drawing butterflies together. Maryam felt happy that she had chosen kind words.

Later, Maryam saw Sara and Amina again. She walked up to them and said, "I'm sorry for interrupting your conversation yesterday. I didn't mean to make you feel uncomfortable." Sara and Amina smiled, and Sara replied, "It's okay, Maryam. We know you didn't mean it, but it's nice that you apologized."

From then on, Maryam made sure to think before speaking. She would pause and ask herself, "Are my words kind? Will they make others feel good?" She found that when she chose her words carefully, her friends were happier, and so was she.

That afternoon, their teacher, Miss Hana, praised Maryam, saying, "I noticed how kind you were to Noor today, Maryam. You practiced Hifz al-Lisan by choosing your words wisely. That's a very important lesson."

Maryam felt proud and knew that guarding her tongue was crucial to keeping her friendships strong and making her world a kinder place.

Moral of the Story: Always think before you speak, choosing words that are kind and thoughtful, because they can make a big difference to others.

Chapter 38

The Blessing of Water: Not Wasting It - Ni'mah

Ahmed loved playing with water. He enjoyed filling up balloons, splashing in the pool, and even spraying his friends with the garden hose. One hot afternoon, he was outside with the hose, making puddles on the ground. He let the water run and run, watching it flow down the street.

His father saw him and called out, "Ahmed, remember to turn off the hose when you're not using it." Ahmed laughed and replied, "But I'm having fun, Baba! There's so much water!"

Later that evening, Ahmed was brushing his teeth. He left the tap running while he brushed, letting the water flow into the sink. His mother walked by and gently turned off the tap, saying, "Ahmed, don't waste water. It's a blessing, a **'Ni'mah'** from Allah."

Ahmed didn't think much about it. He thought water would always be there whenever he wanted it. But the next day at school, Ahmed's teacher, Miss Fatima, spoke about the importance of water. She said, "Water is a precious gift. We use it for drinking, cooking, cleaning, and helping plants grow. In some places, people don't have enough water."

Ahmed was surprised. He had never thought about water like that before. He always thought there was plenty for everyone.

That afternoon, while playing soccer in the park, Ahmed noticed a small sign by the water fountain. It said, "Save water, save life." He wondered what it meant. Just then, he saw an elderly gardener watering the plants carefully, using only a small amount of water for each flower.

Ahmed walked over and asked, "Why do you use so little water?" The gardener smiled and replied, "Water is precious, my boy. We should use only what we need and save the rest. That way, there's enough for everyone, including the plants, animals, and people."

Ahmed thought about this as he walked home. He remembered how he had let the water run while playing and brushing his teeth. He realized he hadn't been careful with this blessing, or Ni'mah, from Allah.

The next day, Ahmed decided to make a change. When he brushed his teeth, he turned off the tap while brushing. He also told his little sister, "Let's only use the water we need!" She smiled and agreed.

Later, while playing outside, he used a bucket to water the plants instead of the hose. His father noticed and said, "Good job, Ahmed! I'm proud of you for saving water."

Ahmed felt happy. He realized that saving water wasn't just about doing less; it was about being thankful for what they had. He understood that every drop was a blessing and that he could make a big difference by using it wisely.

From that day on, Ahmed was careful with water. He made sure to always turn off the taps, use only what was needed, and remind others to do the same. He knew that by conserving water, he was respecting Allah's precious gift.

Moral of the Story: Always conserve water and use it wisely because it is a precious blessing from Allah that we must not waste.

Chapter 39

Visiting the Sick: A Sunnah of Compassion - Iyadah

Zarah was excited about the upcoming school picnic. She had been looking forward to it all week, planning what to bring and imagining the games she would play with her friends. But on the morning of the picnic, Zarah noticed that her friend Aisha was not at school.

During lunch, Zarah asked her teacher, Miss Hana, "Where is Aisha today?" Miss Hana replied, "Aisha is not feeling well. She has a fever and had to stay home."

Zarah felt sad hearing this. She knew how much Aisha had been looking forward to the picnic, just like she was. Later that day, Zarah's mother noticed she looked a little worried and asked, "What's wrong, Zarah?"

Zarah explained, "Aisha is sick, and she missed the picnic. I feel sad for her."

Her mother smiled gently and said, "Zarah, did you know that visiting a sick person is a beautiful Sunnah called '**Iyadah**'? It means offering comfort and support during tough times. It can make someone feel much better, just knowing that you care."

Zarah thought about this and decided she wanted to visit Aisha. Her mother helped her prepare a small basket with fruits, a card, and Aisha's favorite chocolates.

When they arrived at Aisha's house, Zarah felt a little nervous. But when Aisha's mother opened the door and welcomed them in, Zarah felt better. She walked into Aisha's room and saw her friend lying in bed, looking tired.

Zarah gently placed the basket on the table beside Aisha and said, "I brought you some fruits and chocolates. I'm sorry you missed the picnic. We all missed you today." Aisha's face brightened with a smile. "Thank you, Zarah! That's so kind of you," she said softly.

Zarah sat beside Aisha and told her all about the picnic, the fun games they played, and the snacks they shared. She made sure to talk slowly and cheerfully, so Aisha could enjoy the stories even though she was feeling weak.

Aisha giggled when Zarah shared a funny moment from the picnic. For a while, Aisha forgot about her fever and enjoyed her friend's company. Zarah felt happy seeing Aisha smile and knew she had made her friend feel better.

When it was time to leave, Zarah said, "I hope you get well soon, Aisha. We all miss you at school." Aisha nodded and whispered, "Thank you, Zarah. Your visit made me feel much better."

On the way home, Zarah's mother hugged her and said, "I'm so proud of you, Zarah. You practiced Iyadah by visiting Aisha and showing her love and care. The Prophet Muhammad (peace be upon him) taught us that visiting the sick brings blessings to both the visitor and the person who is unwell."

Zarah felt proud and happy. She realized that even a small act of kindness, like visiting a sick friend, could make a big difference.

From that day on, Zarah remembered the importance of Iyadah. She knew that offering comfort and support during tough times was a special way to show love and compassion to others.

Moral of the Story: Always visit and offer comfort to those who are sick, as it shows kindness and brings happiness to their hearts.

Chapter 40

Quiet in the Mosque: Respecting Allah's House - Adab al-Masjid

Yusuf was excited to go to the mosque with his father for the Friday prayers. He loved seeing his friends there and playing in the courtyard after the prayers were over. As they walked into the mosque, Yusuf saw many people quietly sitting and praying.

When Yusuf entered, he felt full of energy. He ran down the hallway, his footsteps echoing loudly. He saw his friend Ali sitting with his father, and he shouted, "Ali, come play with me!" The sound bounced off the walls, and several people turned to look. Yusuf didn't notice; he just wanted to have fun.

Yusuf's father gently placed a hand on his shoulder and said, "Yusuf, remember where we are. This is the mosque, a place of worship. We must show **'Adab al-Masjid'**, which means respect for Allah's house."

Yusuf looked around and saw people praying quietly, some with their hands raised in Dua. He felt a little embarrassed but still didn't quite understand why he needed to be so quiet.

During the prayer, Yusuf sat next to his father, but he couldn't stay still. He fidgeted and whispered to Ali, who was sitting nearby. Ali tried to ignore him, but Yusuf kept poking him. Finally, an older man gently turned and whispered, "Yusuf, please remember that the mosque is a place where people talk to Allah. It's important to stay calm and quiet."

After the prayer, Yusuf's father took him aside. He said, "Yusuf, do you know why we must be quiet and respectful in the mosque?" Yusuf shook his head.

His father explained, "The mosque is Allah's house, a special place where we pray and speak to Allah. It's a place of peace and reflection. When we are noisy or restless, we disturb others who are praying. Showing Adab al-Masjid means behaving calmly, speaking softly, and remembering that this is a place of worship."

Yusuf thought about this and felt a little ashamed. He realized that his loud voice and fidgeting might have disturbed those who were praying.

The next Friday, Yusuf decided to try harder. As they entered the mosque, he walked quietly beside his father. He saw his friends but waved at them with a smile instead of shouting. When he sat down, he folded his hands in his lap and tried to stay still. He watched his father pray with his head bowed and his eyes closed, and he tried to do the same.

During the prayer, Yusuf felt a sense of peace and calm that he hadn't noticed before. He listened to the soft sound of the Imam's voice and felt closer to Allah. After the prayer, his father smiled and whispered, "I'm proud of you, Yusuf. You showed great Adab al-Masjid today."

Yusuf felt proud too. He realized that respecting the mosque didn't just mean being quiet; it meant understanding the special purpose of the place and behaving in a way that honored it.

From then on, Yusuf always remembered to enter the mosque with calmness and respect, knowing that it was a place for worship and peace.

Moral of the Story: Always behave calmly and respectfully in the mosque, as it is a special place for worship and connection with Allah.

Chapter 41

Learning with Love: The Importance of Knowledge - Ilm

Aliya loved going to school and spending time with her friends, but sometimes, she felt bored during her lessons. One day, her teacher, Miss Samira, asked the class, "Can anyone tell me how plants grow?" Aliya shrugged. She didn't know, and she wasn't sure why it mattered.

After school, Aliya's mother noticed she seemed uninterested and asked, "What did you learn today?" Aliya sighed, "Oh, just things about plants. But why do I need to know all that?"

Her mother smiled and said, "Aliya, seeking knowledge, or **'Ilm'**, is very important in Islam. It helps us understand the world that Allah has created. Every bit of knowledge is like a small piece of a big puzzle."

Aliya thought about what her mother said, but she still wasn't sure how learning about plants would help her.

The next day, Miss Samira announced, "We're going on a nature walk today to learn more about plants and trees." Aliya wasn't too excited, but she went along with her class. As they walked through the garden, Miss Samira pointed to a small flower and said, "This flower grows because it gets sunlight, water, and nutrients from the soil."

Aliya watched the flower swaying in the breeze and started to feel curious. She wondered how sunlight and water could help a tiny flower grow tall and beautiful. She raised her hand and asked, "Miss Samira, why do some plants need more water than others?"

Miss Samira smiled and said, "That's a great question, Aliya! Different plants need different amounts of water based on where they grow and what they need to survive. By learning about these things, we understand how to take care of Allah's creations."

Aliya began to feel excited about learning. She bent down to look closer at the different plants. She noticed the shapes of the leaves, the colors of the flowers, and how some plants grew tall while others stayed low to the ground.

At home, Aliya found a book about plants and began reading. She learned that plants not only make food from sunlight but also give us oxygen to breathe. She felt amazed at how everything in Allah's world was connected.

A few days later, Aliya's father showed her the night sky and said, "Do you know the names of any of these stars?" Aliya shook her head. "No, but I'd like to learn!" she replied eagerly. Her father smiled and said, "That's wonderful! The stars have their own stories, just like the plants.

Seeking knowledge helps us see the beauty in everything Allah has created."

Aliya felt excited. She realized that every bit of knowledge was a way to understand the world better. She decided to start asking more questions and paying attention in class. She even began to keep a small notebook to write down everything she wanted to learn about.

From then on, Aliya always remembered the value of Ilm. She knew that seeking knowledge wasn't just about school; it was about discovering all the amazing things Allah had created.

Moral of the Story: Always seek knowledge with love and curiosity, for it helps us understand the world that Allah has created.

Chapter 42

A Clean Heart: Avoiding Jealousy and Hatred - Niyah

Zainab loved to play with her friends in the schoolyard. One day, during recess, she noticed that her friend, Fatima, had a brand-new shiny bicycle. It was bright red with colorful ribbons on the handles. All the children gathered around Fatima, admiring her new bike.

Zainab felt a tight feeling in her chest. She wanted a new bicycle too, but her parents had said they couldn't buy one right now. As she watched Fatima showing off her bike, Zainab's face turned into a frown. She thought, "Why does Fatima get a new bike and not me?"

Later, during class, Zainab sat quietly, still feeling upset. She found it hard to focus on her lessons. She couldn't stop thinking about Fatima's new bike. At lunch, she sat away from her friends, feeling a little angry inside.

Her teacher, Miss Leila, noticed that Zainab looked sad and came over. "Zainab, is everything okay?" Miss Leila asked gently. Zainab hesitated, then replied, "I'm just feeling a bit jealous. Fatima got a new bicycle, and I don't have one."

Miss Leila nodded and smiled kindly. "Zainab, it's normal to feel that way sometimes, but remember that having a clean heart, or '**Niyah**', means keeping it free from jealousy and hatred. When we let these feelings grow, they can make us unhappy and keep us from being good friends."

Zainab thought about Miss Leila's words and realized she didn't want to feel upset or angry with her friend. She wanted to feel happy and have fun with everyone.

That afternoon, when Zainab saw Fatima again, she decided to make a change. She walked over to her and said, "Fatima, your new bike is so beautiful! I'm happy for you." Fatima's face lit up with a big smile. "Thank you, Zainab! Would you like to take a ride on it?"

Zainab was surprised but also felt a warm feeling in her heart. "Really? I would love that!" she replied. Fatima nodded, and they took turns riding the bike around the playground. Zainab laughed and felt happy, forgetting all about her earlier feelings.

Later, Zainab thought about how her feelings had changed. She realized that by letting go of her jealousy, she felt much lighter and happier. She learned that keeping her heart pure and free from jealousy allowed her to enjoy her time with her friends.

The next day, Zainab noticed her friend Aisha looking sad. She asked, "What's wrong, Aisha?" Aisha sighed, "I didn't do well on my math test, and I feel bad." Zainab smiled and said, "Don't worry, Aisha. I can help you study, and we can do better next time together!"

Aisha felt better and thanked Zainab for her kindness. Zainab realized that when she kept her heart pure, free from jealousy and hatred, she could spread more love and happiness to others.

From that day on, Zainab always tried to keep her heart clean, practicing Niyah, by being kind, avoiding jealousy, and celebrating her friends' happiness.

Moral of the Story: Keep your heart clean from jealousy and hatred, as it brings happiness and makes you a better friend.

Chapter 43

Gentle with the Young: The Sunnah of Caring - Rifq al-Sighar

Omar loved playing outside with his friends after school. One sunny afternoon, while they were playing soccer, his little sister, Amina, came running over. "Can I play too?" she asked with a big smile.

Omar felt annoyed. "No, Amina, you're too small. You'll just slow us down," he replied sharply. Amina's smile faded, and she walked away, looking sad. Omar didn't think much about it; he wanted to focus on his game.

Later that day, when Omar got home, he saw Amina struggling to reach a book on a high shelf. She looked at him with hopeful eyes and said, "Omar, can you help me?" But Omar was busy playing with his toys. He quickly said, "I'm too busy, Amina. Find another book to read."

Amina sighed and sat down quietly. Omar's mother noticed and came over. She said softly, "Omar, do you know about '**Rifq al-Sighar**'? It means being gentle and caring with the young, just like our beloved Prophet Muhammad (PBUH) always was."

Omar looked at his mother, feeling a little curious. "But why should I do that, Mama?" he asked.

His mother smiled and explained, "The Prophet Muhammad (PBUH) always treated children with kindness and love. He understood that they are small and need care and patience. When we are gentle with the young, we follow his Sunnah and show love to Allah's little ones."

Omar thought about his mother's words. He felt a little guilty for being impatient with Amina. He decided he would try to be gentler and kinder the next time.

The next day, while playing in the yard, Amina came over again and asked, "Can I play with you, Omar?" This time, Omar remembered what his mother had said. He smiled and said, "Of course, Amina! You can be on my team. Let me show you how to kick the ball."

Amina's face brightened with joy. Omar gently showed her how to kick the ball, and they played together. To his surprise, Amina learned quickly and was having a lot of fun. Omar realized it felt nice to play together and that being gentle with his little sister made them both happy.

Later, when they were at home, Omar saw Amina trying to build a tall tower with her blocks. The tower kept falling, and she looked frustrated. Omar remembered the importance of Rifq al-Sighar. He went over and said, "Let me help you, Amina." He carefully showed her how to stack the blocks so they wouldn't fall.

Amina clapped her hands with joy when they finished the tower. "Thank you, Omar! You're the best!" she said, hugging him. Omar felt a warm feeling in his heart. He realized that being gentle and caring made Amina feel loved and happy.

From that day on, Omar always tried to show kindness and care to Amina and other younger kids. He knew that being gentle, or practicing Rifq al-Sighar, was not only the right thing to do but also made everyone feel better.

Moral of the Story: Be gentle and caring with younger children, as it brings happiness to them and follows the beautiful example of the Prophet Muhammad (Sallallahu Alayhi Wasallam).

Chapter 44

Respecting Property: A Lesson in Integrity - Amanah

Ali loved going to school, especially because he enjoyed playing with the colorful crayons in the classroom. One day, he noticed that his friend Zaid had a special box of bright, shiny markers. Ali thought they looked amazing and wished he had some just like them.

During recess, when everyone went outside to play, Ali saw the box of markers lying on Zaid's desk. He looked around to see if anyone was watching. He thought, "Maybe I can borrow them for a little while. I'll just take them home and bring them back tomorrow."

Ali quickly took the markers and put them in his bag. He felt excited about using them, but a small voice in his heart whispered, "Is this the right thing to do?"

The next day, when Ali came to school, he saw Zaid looking very upset. Zaid was searching everywhere, saying, "I can't find my markers! They were right here on my desk." Ali felt a little guilty, but he kept quiet and didn't say anything.

Their teacher, Miss Layla, noticed Zaid's sadness and asked, "What's wrong, Zaid?" Zaid explained, "My special markers are missing, and I don't know where they went."

Miss Layla gently reminded the class, "Remember, we must respect each other's property. If you find something that doesn't belong to you, you should return it. This is called '**Amanah**', which means trust."

Ali felt his cheeks turn red. He realized he had made a mistake by taking Zaid's markers without asking. He knew he had broken the trust, or Amanah, between him and his friend.

That afternoon, during lunch, Ali decided he needed to make things right. He quietly went to Miss Layla and confessed, "Miss Layla, I took Zaid's markers without asking. I thought I would just borrow them, but I know now that it wasn't right. I want to give them back."

Miss Layla smiled and said, "I'm proud of you, Ali, for being honest and understanding the importance of Amanah. Let's give the markers back to Zaid together."

Ali felt a little nervous but also relieved. He went up to Zaid and said, "Zaid, I'm sorry. I took your markers without asking. Here they are. I hope you can forgive me."

Zaid looked surprised but then smiled. "Thank you for returning them, Ali. I was really worried about losing them. Next time, just ask if you want to use them."

Ali felt happy that Zaid had forgiven him. He realized how important it was to respect other people's belongings and to be trustworthy.

From that day on, Ali always remembered to ask for permission before taking anything that didn't belong to him. He knew that by practicing Amanah, he could be a good friend and earn the trust of others.

Moral of the Story: Always respect other people's property and never take anything without permission, as it builds trust and shows integrity.

Chapter 45

Fulfilling Promises: A Trustworthy Muslim - Wafa'

Fatima loved to play with her friends in the park after school. One day, she promised her friend Layla, "Tomorrow, I will bring my new kite, and we can fly it together!" Layla's eyes sparkled with excitement, and she replied, "I can't wait, Fatima! It will be so much fun!"

The next day, as Fatima was getting ready for school, she noticed her favorite toy on the shelf. She got distracted playing with it and completely forgot about her promise to bring the kite. She left the house in a hurry, not realizing that she had left the kite behind.

At recess, Layla ran over to Fatima and asked eagerly, "Did you bring your kite?" Fatima suddenly remembered her promise and felt a pang of guilt. She shook her head and said, "Oh, I forgot! I'm sorry, Layla."

Layla's smile faded, and she looked disappointed. "But you promised, Fatima," she said quietly. Fatima felt bad, but she quickly said, "I'll bring it tomorrow, I promise!"

The next day, Fatima was in a rush to finish her homework before going to the park. She was so focused on her work that she forgot to pack the kite again. When she met Layla, she saw that her friend looked hopeful. "Did you bring it today?" Layla asked.

Fatima realized she had broken her promise again. She felt ashamed and didn't know what to say. Layla looked sad and walked away quietly. Fatima knew she had disappointed her friend.

That evening, Fatima's mother noticed she looked upset and asked, "What's wrong, Fatima?" Fatima explained how she had forgotten to bring the kite twice and how sad Layla seemed. Her mother gently said, "Fatima, keeping a promise is very important in Islam. It's called '**Wafa**''. When we keep our promises, people trust us and know that we are reliable."

Fatima nodded, understanding now. She decided that the next day, she would not forget. Before going to bed, she placed the kite right next to her school bag to make sure she would remember.

The next morning, Fatima picked up the kite first thing and put it in her bag. She felt determined to fulfill her promise this time. At school, she couldn't wait for recess. As soon as the bell rang, she ran over to Layla and said, "Look! I brought the kite today, just like I promised!"

Layla's face lit up with joy. "Really? Thank you, Fatima!" she exclaimed. They both ran to the park and took turns flying the kite. It soared high in the sky, and both girls laughed and cheered.

Fatima felt proud that she had kept her promise. She saw how happy Layla was, and she knew she had done the right thing. She realized that by practicing Wafa', she was showing that she could be trusted.

From that day on, Fatima made sure to always keep her promises. She learned that fulfilling her promises made her a trustworthy friend, and it also made her feel happy inside.

Moral of the Story: Always keep your promises, because it shows you are trustworthy and dependable, and it makes others happy.

Chapter 46

Gratitude in Hard Times: A Story of Faith - Shukr al-Haal

Musa was excited about the big soccer game after school. He had been practicing for weeks and felt ready to help his team win. But just before the game, dark clouds gathered, and heavy rain began to pour. The teacher announced, "The game is canceled due to the weather."

Musa felt disappointed and upset. "Why did it have to rain today?" he thought. He had been looking forward to this game so much. As he walked home, he felt sad and angry, kicking small stones along the way.

When he got home, his mother noticed his unhappy face and asked, "What's wrong, Musa?" Musa sighed, "The soccer game got canceled because of the rain. I was really excited to play, but now everything is ruined."

His mother listened carefully and then said, "Musa, do you know about **'Shukr al-Haal'**? It means being grateful to Allah, even when things don't go the way we want." Musa frowned and asked, "But how can I be grateful when I'm feeling so disappointed?"

His mother smiled gently and said, "Think about the rain, Musa. It may have spoiled your game today, but it also waters the plants, fills the rivers, and brings coolness after a hot day. Allah knows what is best for us, even if we don't always understand it."

Musa thought about his mother's words but still felt a bit upset. He decided to try and think of something he was grateful for. He remembered that the rain meant he could spend time with his family. That evening, they all sat together and played a fun board game. Musa began to feel a little better, realizing that he was having a good time with his family.

The next day, Musa woke up with a sore throat. He felt tired and weak. His father took him to the doctor, who said, "You have a cold, Musa. You'll need to rest for a few days." Musa felt disappointed again. "Now I can't play outside or see my friends," he thought.

But then Musa remembered his mother's words about Shukr al-Haal. He decided to practice gratitude. He thought, "I may not feel well, but I'm thankful for the warm soup my mom made for me and the cozy blanket I have." He realized that even though he felt sick, there were still things to be grateful for.

Over the next few days, Musa rested, drank plenty of water, and got better. When he finally returned to school, his friends were happy to see him, and the teacher announced that the soccer game had been rescheduled for next week.

Musa smiled, feeling happy that he would get another chance to play. He realized that being grateful, even in hard times, had helped him feel better and see the good in every situation.

From that day on, Musa practiced Shukr al-Haal by finding something to be thankful for, no matter what happened. He knew that gratitude brought peace to his heart and helped him stay strong in faith.

Moral of the Story: Always remain grateful to Allah, even when things don't go your way, because gratitude brings happiness and peace.

Chapter 47

Don't Waste Food: The Story of Blessings – Ni'mat al-Ta'am

Yara loved snacks. She would often fill her plate with chips, cookies, and candies, enjoying the tasty treats after school. However, she also had a habit of taking more than she could eat. When she got full, she would leave the rest, thinking nothing of it.

One afternoon, Yara's family visited her grandmother. When they arrived, her grandmother was preparing a delicious lunch of lentil soup, bread, and fruit. Yara filled her plate with a big serving of soup and extra bread, but halfway through, she pushed her bowl away and said, "I'm done! I don't want any more."

Her grandmother noticed the leftover food and asked softly, "Yara, why did you take so much if you weren't going to finish it?"

Yara shrugged and replied, "I thought I was hungrier, Grandma. There's still a lot of food, so it's okay."

Her grandmother smiled gently and said, "Yara, do you know that in my village, there were times when we had very little to eat? Every bit of food was precious. We thanked Allah for each bite and made sure not to waste anything."

Yara looked at her grandmother curiously. "Really? What did you do if there wasn't enough?" she asked.

Her grandmother nodded and continued, "We would share whatever little we had. We learned to value each grain of rice and every piece of bread. Food is a gift from Allah, or **'Ni'mat al-Ta'am'**, and we must use it wisely."

Yara felt a bit embarrassed. She hadn't thought about food that way before. She looked down at her plate and realized how much she had wasted. "I'm sorry, Grandma," she said softly. "I didn't mean to waste the food."

Her grandmother smiled and said, "It's okay, Yara. Now you know. Let's make a promise to only take what we can eat and appreciate every meal as a blessing from Allah."

Yara nodded, feeling determined. She decided to finish the rest of her food, even though she wasn't that hungry. It made her realize that every bite counted.

A few days later, Yara went to the park with her friend, Hana. They brought a picnic lunch with sandwiches, apples, and juice. Hana began to peel her apple and dropped the peel on the ground. Yara quickly said, "Hana, don't waste the peel! We can put it in the compost bin to help plants grow!"

Hana looked surprised but agreed, saying, "You're right, Yara. We shouldn't waste anything."

Yara felt happy knowing that she was being mindful of her blessings. She enjoyed her picnic, making sure nothing was left behind. Even the crumbs were brushed away for the birds.

From then on, Yara always remembered her grandmother's words. She appreciated every meal, big or small, and made sure not to waste food, knowing it was a precious gift from Allah.

Moral of the Story: Always respect food and avoid wasting it, as it is a blessing from Allah and should be valued with gratitude.

Chapter 48

Helping Your Siblings: The Bond of Brotherhood - Ukhuwwah

Hasan and Malik were brothers, but they were very different. Hasan loved to read books and draw pictures, while Malik enjoyed building things with his blocks and playing outside. Sometimes, they didn't always agree on what to do, and it led to small arguments.

One day, Hasan was busy drawing a picture for an art contest at school. He was using his favorite colors and carefully adding details to make it look beautiful. Meanwhile, Malik was trying to build a tall tower with his blocks. But every time he stacked the blocks higher, they kept falling over. He grew frustrated and called out, "Hasan, can you help me, please?"

Hasan glanced over but was too focused on his drawing. "Not now, Malik. I'm busy," he replied, without looking up.

Malik felt a bit sad but decided to try again. The tower kept collapsing, and he felt like giving up. A few moments later, Hasan finished his drawing and looked over at Malik's sad face. He remembered how the Prophet Muhammad (PBUH) taught the importance of **'Ukhuwwah'**, or brotherhood, which means helping and supporting each other.

Hasan walked over to Malik and said, "I'm sorry, Malik. Let me help you with your tower." Malik's face brightened, and together they carefully placed the blocks one by one. Hasan showed Malik how to balance them, and soon, the tower stood tall and steady.

Malik jumped up with joy and hugged Hasan. "Thank you, Hasan! You're the best brother!" he said. Hasan felt happy seeing his brother smile and realized how good it felt to help.

The next day, it was Malik's turn to help. Hasan was trying to reach a book on a high shelf. He stretched on his toes but couldn't quite reach it. Malik noticed and quickly grabbed a small stool. He climbed up and got the book for Hasan.

"Here you go, Hasan!" Malik said with a big grin. Hasan took the book and said, "Thank you, Malik! That was very helpful."

Throughout the week, they continued to help each other with little things—sharing their toys, helping clean up their room, and even helping each other with homework. They realized that when they worked together, everything seemed easier and more fun.

One afternoon, their mother noticed how nicely they were playing together and said, "I'm so proud of both of you for practicing Ukhuwwah. You're showing what it means to be loving and supportive brothers."

Hasan and Malik looked at each other and smiled. They knew they were becoming better brothers by helping and supporting one another.

From that day on, whenever one of them needed help, the other was always there. They learned that by practicing Ukhuwwah, they were strengthening their bond of brotherhood and growing closer every day.

Moral of the Story: Always help and support your siblings, as it strengthens your bond of love and makes everyone happier.

Chapter 49

Don't Be Greedy: Sharing What You Love - Ithar

Ali loved his toy cars more than anything. He had a collection of all sorts—red, blue, green, big, small, and even one that could light up and make sounds. After school, Ali would line up his cars on the floor and play for hours, racing them back and forth.

One sunny afternoon, Ali's friend, Omar, came over to play. Omar saw the colorful cars and his eyes widened with excitement. "Wow, Ali! Can I play with your cars too?" he asked eagerly.

Ali hesitated. He loved his cars and didn't like anyone else touching them. He frowned and said, "No, these are my cars. You can play with the blocks instead."

Omar looked disappointed but agreed to play with the blocks. After a while, Ali noticed that Omar seemed bored. He felt a little bad, but he didn't want to share his favorite toys. He thought, "Why should I share my cars? They are mine."

Later that day, Ali's mother gave him a delicious chocolate bar. Ali loved chocolates and couldn't wait to eat it. Just as he was about to take a bite, his little sister, Fatima, came over and said, "Ali, can I have a piece too?"

Ali shook his head. "No, this is mine," he said quickly. Fatima looked sad but walked away quietly. Ali took a big bite of the chocolate but didn't feel as happy as he thought he would.

That evening, Ali's father noticed Ali was quiet and asked, "What's on your mind, Ali?" Ali explained how he didn't want to share his toys or his chocolate. His father nodded and said, "Ali, do you know about **'Ithar'**?"

Ali shook his head. His father continued, "Ithar means putting others before yourself. It's about sharing what you love and being selfless. When we share, we make others happy, and that brings more joy to our hearts."

Ali thought about this. He decided to try to practice Ithar the next day.

When Omar came over again, Ali smiled and said, "Omar, would you like to play with my cars today?" Omar's face lit up with joy. "Really? Thank you, Ali!" he exclaimed.

They played with the cars together, racing them and laughing. Ali realized he was having more fun playing with his friend than he ever did alone. It felt good to share.

Later, when Fatima asked again for a piece of his chocolate, Ali smiled and said, "Here, Fatima, you can have half." Fatima's face brightened up with a big smile, and she hugged Ali. "Thank you, Ali! You're the best brother!" she said.

Ali felt a warm feeling in his heart. He realized that sharing his favorite things brought him more happiness than keeping them all to himself.

From that day on, Ali practiced Ithar by sharing his toys, snacks, and even his time with others. He learned that selflessness brought joy not just to others, but also to himself.

Moral of the Story: Always share what you love with others, as selflessness brings joy and happiness to everyone around you.

Chapter 50

The Art of Apology: Saying Sorry When Wrong - Tawbah

Mariam loved playing on the playground with her friends, especially on the big, red slide. One sunny day, Mariam and her friends, Noor and Hana, decided to play a game of tag. Mariam was "it" and ran around, trying to catch her friends.

As they ran around the playground, Mariam saw Noor climbing up the ladder to the slide. Mariam thought this was her chance. She sprinted over quickly, hoping to tag Noor before she could slide down. But in her excitement, Mariam accidentally pushed Noor from behind, a bit too hard. Noor lost her balance, stumbled, and fell to the ground, scraping her knee. Tears welled up in Noor's eyes, and she started to cry.

Mariam stopped and felt her heart sink. She hadn't meant to hurt Noor; she just wanted to win the game. But instead of helping Noor or asking if she was okay, Mariam quickly said, "It wasn't my fault! You shouldn't have been in the way!"

Noor's face showed a mixture of pain and sadness. Hana quickly rushed over to help Noor up. Noor's knee was bleeding a little, and she looked hurt, both in her knee and in her feelings. She whispered through her tears, "I didn't mean to be in the way, Mariam. I was just trying to play."

For the rest of the day, Noor stayed quiet, keeping her distance from Mariam. Even though they were friends, Noor felt sad and hurt by Mariam's words and actions. Meanwhile, Mariam couldn't help but feel a tight knot in her stomach. She knew she had done something wrong—not just by pushing Noor, but also by not saying sorry when Noor needed her to.

Mariam remembered what she had learned about '**Tawbah**', which means sincerely apologizing when you make a mistake and asking for forgiveness. She thought about how she would feel if someone had pushed her and then didn't say sorry. She realized that Noor must be feeling very sad and upset.

That evening, when Mariam went home, her mother noticed her frown and asked, "Is something wrong, Mariam?" Mariam hesitated, then told her mother everything that had happened with Noor. Her mother listened carefully and said, "Mariam, everyone makes mistakes, but it's important to say sorry and mean it. Tawbah teaches us that a sincere apology shows we understand our mistake and want to make things right."

Mariam nodded, feeling determined. She decided she would apologize to Noor the very next day and make things right.

The next morning, when Mariam arrived at school, she spotted Noor sitting alone on a bench. Mariam took a deep breath and walked over, feeling nervous but knowing this was the right thing to do. She gently sat down beside Noor and said, "Noor, I am so sorry for pushing you yesterday. I didn't mean to hurt you, and I'm sorry I didn't help you or say sorry right away. Will you forgive me?"

Noor looked at Mariam with surprise, then her face softened into a smile. "It's okay, Mariam. I know you didn't mean to hurt me. Thank you for saying sorry," she said, wiping away a small tear. They hugged, and Noor's smile grew brighter.

That day, they played together again on the playground, laughing and having fun like always. Mariam felt a warm happiness in her heart, knowing that she had made things right with her friend. She realized that saying sorry when you're wrong wasn't just about fixing a mistake—it was about showing you care and respecting others' feelings.

From that day on, Mariam always remembered the lesson of Tawbah. She knew that a sincere apology could mend a friendship, heal hearts, and show true strength and kindness.

Moral of the Story: Always apologize sincerely when you make a mistake, as it shows kindness, respect, and makes friendships stronger.

www.ingramcontent.com/pod-product-compliance
Lightning Source LLC
Chambersburg PA
CBHW051210290426
44109CB00021B/2405